Wel-come to India

Wel-come to India

CHRISTOPHER CORR
& EAMONN LEDDY

MACDONALD ORBIS

For Pauline, who would have loved India.

A *Macdonald Orbis* BOOK

© Eamonn Leddy & Christopher Corr 1988

First published in Great Britain in 1988
by Macdonald & Co (Publishers) Ltd
London & Sydney

A member of Maxwell Pergamon Publishing Corporation plc

British Library Cataloguing in Publication Data
Leddy, Eamonn
  Wel-come to India.
  I. India – (Republic). Description & travel
  – Personal observations
  I. Title   II. Corr, Christopher
  915.4′0452

  ISBN 0–356–15675–3

Filmset by Wyvern Typesetting Ltd
Printed and bound in Great Britain
by Purnell Book Production, a member of BPCC plc

Senior Editor: Catherine Rubinstein
Senior Art Editor: Clive Hayball
Designer: Ann Braybon
Design Assistant: Mark Davies
Photography: Susanna Price and Jon Bouchier

The authors are grateful for the kind assistance of
the Curwen Gallery, London W1.

Macdonald & Co (Publishers) Ltd
Greater London House
Hampstead Road
London NW1 7QX

Contents

'Namaste' 6

'India Proper' – the Deccan Plateau 12

Gujarat 28

Rajasthan 52

The Northern Plains 70

Darjeeling and Nepal 94

The foothills of the Himalayas 104

Drawing in India 124

Index 128

'Namaste'

6th January – Bombay

AT 6.20 A.M. LOCAL TIME we touchdown in darkness at Bombay Airport. I join the palms of my hands, turn to Chris and say 'Namaste' (the literal Sanskrit meaning, 'I bow to the God in you', is rather more formal and extreme in its humility than our lifelong friendship requires, but it's the most common form of greeting all over the subcontinent and is apparently an appropriate form of salutation between all castes and ranks of people). We have practised it many times before on our weekend Hindi course in Tower Hamlets,

'NAMASTE'

which also taught us how to 'interrogate' unsuspecting Hindi speakers to acquire such useful information as the names of their spinster aunt's (on their mother's side) second cousins, where they lived, when they were born, what their occupations were and how many brothers and sisters they had. It could have been called 'So you think you want to become an Immigration Officer?'.

At 7.30 a.m. we step out of the airport building into bright sunshine and a swarm of taxi-drivers, beggars, sweepers. . . . We struggle with our bags onto the wrong bus and have to get off again in a hurry. It is already very warm. The airport car park is full of big rounded Hindustan 'Ambassadors', made in Calcutta and resembling early 1950s Morris Oxfords with a three-pointed-trident, symbol of Shiva, on the bonnet. My old Volvo would be very much at home here.

The moving scene through the bus window on the ride into the city is a feature-length film. On the edge of parched fields a thin line of shanty huts clings to the roadside. There are people everywhere. Dark men and boys in long and short 'skirts', called lungis, sit by stalls and makeshift cafés doing nothing except spitting out streams of red betel nut juice, blowing their noses on the street or shitting by the roadside. Others are waiting for buses, dodging cows, riding bicycles, driving bullock carts and auto-rickshaws. Horn honking is incessant and obligatory for all classes of vehicle. After ten minutes of this mayhem we are completely overwhelmed and exhausted.

We pass strawmat houses and homes made in huge cylindrical concrete pipes. Gradually the shanty becomes a city of solid thirties art deco style buildings with coloured glass windows, curved frontages and cut-out ornamental facades in peeling painted stucco. There are still people asleep on the pavements as the shops open up. The incredible noise of the traffic steadily increases in volume. Suddenly we reach the Arabian Sea. Pilgrims file up and down past squatting beggars on a long causeway to Haji Ali's tomb (a Moslem saint who drowned here). Opposite is the busiest racecourse in India. We pass the Hanging Gardens, behind which rise the Parsis' Towers of Silence where they lay out their dead for the vultures to pick clean. The Parsis do not bury or cremate their dead

PAN STALL

because they hold fire, earth and water sacred.

We walk up Mahatma Gandhi Road through the Maidan, where we see our first performing mongoose and some 'dhaba-wallahs' with 'meals-on-wheels' pushcarts playing their part in the complicated process which ensures that thousands of business commuters get their home-made lunch delivered to their offices in multi-compartmented colour-coded metal 'lunch boxes'. Past the Gymkhana Sports Club with cricket pavilions, tennis courts and swimming pool (Pukka officers' class) stands Victoria Terminus, Bombay's huge Gothic railway station, just like St Pancras. Chris starts to draw and is surrounded by station porters wearing

red jackets, red turbans and brass licence discs on armbands. The trains pull in, full to bursting with passengers hanging out of the open doors. Men in cotton check shirts with huge bundles and baskets on their heads weave quickly and gracefully through the crowds. There are vendors and shoe-shiners everywhere. Opposite the station families are living on the street in reed tents and tin huts, cooking over open fires.

Just up the road by the open-air barber stalls is Mahatma Phule market. Beyond the stench of the meat hall is a most beautiful area selling fruit and vegetables – huge mounds of pineapples, oranges and sugar cane. Sunlight streams through the gaps in the strung-up sacking. The floor is 6 in deep in straw. We are entranced by the constant procession of handsome porters in lungis carrying huge flat baskets on their heads. Some porters are lying curled up in their empty baskets like cats. A boy in a red turban is sitting cleaning people's ears. He wears a little box of 'tools' around his neck. We feel very self-conscious but muster enough courage in

the midst of many staring faces to take a hurried photo. Several porters quickly pose for us to take another. Chris starts to draw and is instantly besieged by young boys who want to be drawn and photographed. The heat and brightness are intense and we suffer terrible waves of exhaustion. All day long there is no let-up in the hustle and bustle and constant noise. We walk by families living on stairways and under flyovers. Every young woman appears to have several small children. At dusk we sit by the Gateway to India, a triumphal arch commemorating a visit of George V, looking at the display of tiny pleasure craft and huge tankers and merchant ships afloat on the Arabian Sea.

OPPOSITE: FRUIT AND VEGETABLE MARKET

'India Proper'- the Deccan Plateau

8th January – Nasik

W E WAKE WITH THE SUN streaming in. We are covered in mosquito bites, our throats are sore and our noses blocked. Can we have colds, or is it just the dust? Inches thick in the streets, it fills the air and diffuses the light. You can taste it and feel it in every pore.

In a courtyard a woman throws stones at some cows. We walk through an arched gateway into a small market square hemmed in by three-storey

OPPOSITE: CROSSING THE PLAINS

MARKET STALLS

NASIK MARKET

balconied hotels and lodging houses. The pungent scent of burning incense wafts from the flower garland stall and in one area Tibetan refugees sell hand-knitted bright-coloured woollens. Up an alleyway between huge piles of yellow-orange hay, bullock carts stand patiently waiting to be loaded and unloaded. The horns of the cattle are painted bright reds and blues. Women glide by, carrying large baskets on their heads piled high with fresh cow dung to be used as fuel. They will pat it into large buns and stick them to a wall to dry in the sun. Small black-haired pigs snuffle among the piles of bamboo, reeds and grasses.

We sit by the holy Godawari River at the eastern

WOMEN DHOBIS

edge of town. There is so much to look at. Behind us people are selling fruit and spices off mats on the ground. In front of us is the grain-selling area, a hive of activity. Sacks (labelled 'Polish Rock Salt') are unloaded from trucks and pushcarts which have beeped and coaxed their way through the market crush. The buyers and sellers sift and re-sift the grain, discard the chaff and weigh out measures on large wooden tripod scales. Dozens of women are washing clothes in the river and slapping them on the stone banks. A boy stands knee-deep washing his bicycle. Donkeys and cows wander seeming aimless till they suddenly snatch at a pile of tomatoes or carrots and are beaten away. On the opposite river bank two proud drivers are washing their big painted trucks, up to their axles in water.

On the open ground next to them men come and go to relieve their bowels. As it is necessary to rid oneself at one stroke of all the pollutions of the night, that most inauspicious of all times, every Hindu has to start, and does start, his day by relieving himself. The whole of India relieves itself at the same time. The performance lasts an extremely long time and takes place mostly in fields and by road- and rail-sides.

In the distance is a mud-brick works, its stock piled up like ancient fortifications. Constant streams of auto-rickshaws, bullock carts, donkeys, scooters, motorbikes, bicycles and heavily laden and unladen pedestrians crowd the river crossings. Water buffaloes soak in the pools formed by the bridges and walkways. Yesterday's orange, white and yellow marigold garlands float downstream with melon rinds and other rubbish. Herons watch from the opposite bank while large eagles circle overhead. Crowds, mostly kids, gather round Chris as he paints.

Down a back street we are surrounded by young women who eye us up and down rather boldly. They start to giggle and try to grab us and pull us indoors. We escape into a costume and mask shop. The proprietor speaks excellent theatrical English ('Pussy cat, pussy cat where have you been? I've been up to London to visit the Queen . . . .'). He takes us into his showroom and showers us with papier-mâché masks of animals, birds and gods. He regales us with legends from Hindu mythology and is an excellent salesman. We are not very good at bartering yet!

Nearby are the bathing ghats (steps leading into the river where pilgrims cleanse their souls and make 'puja' – worship). There are temples and shrines everywhere. After dark the temples are decorated with fairy lights and taped music comes from a nearby tent. Flower garlands, votive offerings and brightly painted plaster animals and figures are sold from cloth sheets and baskets. On large silver trays are piled cone-shaped mounds of fluorescent coloured powders for marking shrines and foreheads. There is a dimly lit primitive funfair with a hand-operated wooden 'big' wheel and a merry-go-round. In a small outdoor 'gym' athletic

STREET IN KHULTABAD

young men are exercising, weightlifting and swing-ing wildly on a set of parallel bars. And always there is the noise of horns and people shouting. Everybody shouts in India. At us they shout 'Hi!', 'Hello!', 'How are you?', 'What is your name?', 'What is your good country?', 'You are from London proper?'.

The streets are full of 'cupboard shops' open to the street. Later I learn that they are called 'hut-ments'. They sell everything under the sun – books, stationery, pots and pans, cloth, electrical goods, sweets and tobacco. . . . They all have hand-painted shutters and signs. Outrageous signs for doctors and dentists. Formal signs for lawyers and tax advisers . . . and even contact lens specialists!

At the crossroads a brass band dressed in green uniforms marches past followed by a band of drummers and a hand-pulled altar on wheels decorated with candles, flowers and pictures. A very large elephant with a roving trunk slowly brings up the rear, causing a traffic uproar.

Our First Bus Ride

The bus leaves at 6 o'clock. The northern outskirts of Aurangabad are dotted with mosques, walled houses and gardens and Moslem monuments – not what we expected to see at all. The sun has set and before long the light fades. We pass lots of elaborately painted lorries with PUBLIC CARRIER on their fronts. The grilles are painted with geometric patterns and fringes of painted chains hang from the front bumpers. They often drive without side mirrors and with no rear view. On their rear is always painted HORN OK PLEASE – not that the other road users need any such encouragement.

Most auto-rickshaws also have no side mirrors. The sound of their horns varies from a wet fart to a manic donkey. Most bicycles have no bells, and few have lights. They rely on their riders to sound a warning. You must be on constant alert in an Indian street – it seems you can more or less drive anywhere on the road, or off it, as long as you do not hit anything else. The only rule of the road is 'Might is right!' and this means steer clear of the trucks. They are usually heavily overloaded and in poor shape. Indeed they are licensed to carry 25 per cent over the limit recommended by their manufacturer. 'Juggernaut' is originally an Indian word, used for the massive and enormously heavy mobile shrines which worshippers pull dangerously around the streets between important religious sites.

On the buses the ticket collectors aggressively assert their power. They rattle their ticket punches loudly on the rails and shout at passengers to 'Open the window!', 'Close the window!', 'Pay for your ticket!', 'Don't smoke!', 'Move down the bus!', 'Go wash your mouth out!' . . . . Then they turn out all the lights and it's pitch dark. We sit at the back by the exit to make getting off easier but soon realise our mistake. It is the bumpiest part of the bus and the roads are bad enough to shake all your fillings out. We are lifted inches off our seat and on landing are drowned in a sea of dust which rises from our seats and the emergency exit behind us. Beams of light from oncoming traffic stream through the front windows over the silhouetted heads like projector lights in a cinema. As the vehicles pass, the shafts of light sweep through the air like searchlights in the Blitz, illuminating all the particles of dust. It becomes hard to breathe and the constant big dipper leaps stir memories of the rice we had at the bus station before we left. I reach for the sick bag, which is not there. I notice several men have removed their Nehru caps – another of their 1001 uses? I begin to wonder about my bag, which was slung on the roof without being strapped down and was probably flung off after a violent bump several miles back, stunning some roadside squatter and showering him with Sainsbury's toilet rolls, like manna from heaven!

12th January – Ajanta

At 7.15 a.m. Chris opens the door to see what sort of day it is (we have not yet got used to the fact that it is always the same) and is instantly ambushed by a horde of noisy teenage Gujarati schoolchildren who swarm into our room with ghetto blasters playing Western pop and demanding that we breakdance for them. I tell them that I never breakdance before 8.00 on a Monday morning. Chris gives them a false address and promises to write to all 56 of them and visit their English Medium Secondary School in Surat soon.

The caves of Ajanta are famed for their magnificent Buddhist paintings. The caves date from around 200 BC to AD 650 and were only dramatically rediscovered as recently as 1819 by a British hunting party. The pictures are very finely painted over massive areas, incorporating clever techniques – e.g. a painted Buddha seems to be turned to face you whichever side of him you stand; a cow on the ceiling likewise appears to turn upside down completely – whichever side you look up from, it is walking towards you. There are 29 caves. In the last of them is a beautifully carved large reclining Buddha. Three 'gypsy' women enter wearing brightly coloured clothes, lots of bracelets and jewels dangling from small plaits at the sides of their foreheads. A maharaja wearing a long red coat with a curved dagger tucked in to his waistband and a colourful

SACRED COW AND HOOPOE

turban is escorted round by his bodyguards and a site official. The Indian tourists are huddled in groups outside the caves listening to the World Cup cricket on the radio.

In the village we are swamped by children yelling 'Hello! Hello!', 'Pen, baksheesh!'. From two years old upwards they run across streets and fields chanting their incessant litany: 'Hello, hello, what is your name?' 'Hello, hello, pen, baksheesh!' Nothing we say has any effect – the needle is stuck good and proper and it becomes very tiresome.

14th January – Ujjain

We arrived in Indore late last night after an $11\frac{1}{2}$-hour bus journey of about 190 miles, never stopping for more than ten minutes and with the same driver and conductor. We immediately acquired a new 'friend' called Sado, who found us our hotel. He wants to make our minds up for us about how we will spend the next few days. No need to worry, he will arrange everything. Everybody knows him. Money is nothing – only friendship! Do you have

OPPOSITE: TEMPLES IN UJJAIN

any jeans, cameras, coins . . . ? By the way, there was a man here in Indore who gave some foreigners some sweets and they were drugged and when they awoke everything had been stolen. You must not trust anybody! Honesty is the best policy! By the way, would you like a toffee?

Today is the feast of Mankar Sankranti, a kite-flying festival, which marks the end of winter. The nights start shortening and the winds change direction on this date. *The Free Press Journal* contains several nasty stories – 'Leper buried alive by untouchables', 'Tribal girl gang raped' – as well as reports on union disputes, religious disputes, language disputes, water shortages, land productivity problems, concerns over education. . . . *Jewel in the Crown* is on the telly tonight. At the back are pages of marriage ads where handsome graduate bachelors and issueless divorcees (age, height, weight and caste supplied) seek fair (skinned) convent or well-educated girls from respectable families.

In the railway station an old man with a large silver tray of orange and white marigold chains removes yesterday's withered garland from the gaudy picture of a Hindu god in one or other of his many forms and replaces it with a fresh necklace. Chris starts to draw but his view is soon completely blocked by the knees of the curious crowd of onlookers. There is an announcement to stand back from the platform, then WHOOSH! a train hurtles through, creating a miniature dust storm.

Our small-gauge, steam-driven train to Ujjain reminds us of when we were kids – the smell of the smoke, the chug-chug of the engine, the push-pull starting effect. We travel second class on wooden seats with a tier above for sleeping. The 50-mile, two-hour trip costs 4 rupees (25 pence) each. On the bench opposite us sit five middle-aged women in their best travelling garb – long billowing skirts and long matching capes with hoods tied in a bow in dazzling colours – cerise, scarlet, turquoise, pink and aquamarine. Four of them wear thick square-rimmed glasses. They could almost be nuns, but look more like a troupe of drag artistes from Leeds. They share some fruit with us – our first taste of fresh guavas.

We see dusty villages with packs of vultures, mountains of cotton, and dung buns drying in the sun. Red chillies are spread out on blankets in the streets, in the fields and on 'hot' tin roofs. It becomes greener. There are hay-ricks and crowned cranes in the fields and oak trees. We meet a traditional toy maker from Meerut, near Delhi, where the 1857 Mutiny first broke out. When I tell him my name is Irish he proclaims: 'But the Irish killed Mountbatten. We were very shocked. He did a lot of good things for this country.'

Ujjain is happy and calm. Perhaps it's because of the festival. On every rooftop families and groups of children are flying paper kites of many colours and designs. The sky is alive with them, the trees blossom with them. Ujjain has a long and distinguished history and the old town is full of beautiful houses with carved wooden pillars and window-frames. The lintels are decorated with auspicious signs and hung with sacred leaves to drive away ghosts and demons.

We enter a small Hindu temple where a ceremony is in progress – a crescendo of frantic bell-ringing followed by group singing. A boy invites us for a cup of tea across the road. We sit on chairs in the street while Ashoka, who runs the tea

MANDU

stall, proudly makes us tea (water, buffalo milk, sugar and tea are all boiled up together) in front of a small audience.

Ujjain is a holy city for Hindus and all along the banks of the Sipra River are stacked large temple complexes and bathing ghats. The sun sinks below the pink and orange glowing horizon. Saffron-robed penitents with shaved heads make offerings of flowers, light joss sticks and make puja. Others are busy washing themselves and their clothes in the river. A group of cows stand lazily munching bunches of coriander. We listen to the distant hum of the city and snatches of music and watch the darting dots and shadows of kites. As the light fades, dark shapes wing their way up the river and pass low overhead – huge bats the size of crows!

16th January – Mandu

It was already dark last night when we entered the series of gates that protect the sprawling hilltop ghost fort of Mandu. Over a large pot of tea, English style, the 'waiter' at the Government Tourist Bungalow asked me whether Surrey and Sussex and Derbyshire are all parts of 'London proper'. He is crazy about cricket and calls me Mr Geoffrey Boycott, sir! At breakfast I give him a quickly sketched map of England showing where the cricket counties and major towns are. He says he will keep it for ever. He is going to spend all day watching the one-day international on TV between India and Australia in Melbourne.

We wander across the plateau, passing animals and villagers and children who wave and say 'bye-bye'. Everyone is very friendly. Three mongrel dogs adopt us and chaperone us all day. Mandu is littered with monuments and mausoleums. Soon we come across a beautiful mosque and an old caravanserai built in the Moghul era. Hay-laden bullock carts trundle slowly past.

The northern 'Royal' complex contains the sloping-walled Hindola Mahal and the Jahaz Mahal, or 'Ship Palace', with water on either side. Cows and goats graze while women do the washing and groups of men beat the water with sticks, herding fish into the shallows and their nets. We try to imagine the splendour and magnificence of the scene in its heyday – a marvellous array of interconnecting rooms and baths with pools and water channels everywhere, and splendid views of the other palaces. It was really a 16th-century Royal pleasure resort ruled over by Baz Bahadur, the poet prince and patron of the arts, and his consort Rani Roopmati, whose elevated pavilion overlooking the plains to the south can be seen on the horizon from the Jahaz Mahal. The tales of their romance are legendary.

As the sun goes down we walk back through the village that is Mandu today, admiring the strikingly decorated mud houses. Some of the doorways are painted with geometric designs picked out with silver or gold paper. We sit in the ruins of the Asharfi Mahal opposite the imposing many-domed

EVENING TIME IN MANDU VILLAGE

Jami Masjid ('Friday Mosque'). The biggest dome is home to thousands of bats. There is no breeze and the blue smoke from the village fires hangs low over the ground. Women fill beautifully shaped earthenware pots from the green-surfaced water tank behind us, their saris and skirts ablaze with colours – bright violets, lime greens and vibrant fuchsias. Hems sparkle with gold and silver threads. About their ankles and wrists, metal bracelets jangle in counterpoint to the brass bells hung on the bullocks who tread in nearby fields. The sky becomes more vivid as the colours spread to meet each other before fading away below the horizon.

India defeated Australia by eight wickets!

Gujarat

19th January – Ahmadabad

NOISY, POLLUTED AHMADABAD is the centre of the textile industry, the 'Manchester of the East'. Today we visit two museums before breakfast. The first has a wonderful collection of the various schools of Indian miniature paintings in a large Le Corbusier building. The museum attendant follows us round every picture, looking over our shoulders. He is lonely; we are the only visitors in the museum. He tells us the building dates from 1963, '30 years old and designed by a Japanese'. He asks: 'Is it cold in England?', 'Can

GOATHERD IN SAURASHTRA

you earn good money in Kuwait?', 'I have heard that . . .'. Then, bored with our intense concentration on the pictures and apparent lack of concern for his career prospects, he amuses himself by singing loudly his favourite Hindi-Pop songs. There are many beautiful paintings here but they do seem rather neglected, like our singing guard.

The Gujarat Folk and Crafts Museum resembles a hippie museum to the Portobello Road of the sixties. A fabulous display of embroidered, mirrored and beaded skirts, tunics, bags and wall-hangings, paintings on glass, tie-dyed and block-printed fabrics, embroidered stuffed toys and lots of beads and jewellery. The college next door houses a children's museum full of beautiful masks, toys and models. Out on the street gangs of large monkeys with pale grey fur and black faces terrorize the neighbourhood. They bound along, bouncing off cars, knocking over scooters, shaking all the trees and helping themselves to whatever they want. These common langurs are associated with the monkey-god Hanuman, hero of the *Ramayana* stories, and are

OPPOSITE: NIGHT TIME IN AHMADABAD

considered holy and revered by Hindus.

The best way to travel around this big, dusty, colourless city is by auto-rickshaw (three-wheeled covered scooters with seats for two passengers behind the driver). It's like stepping into a Keystone Cops movie. We weave through all the other traffic with horn jammed on and stop for nothing. At crossroads it's best to close your eyes. The drivers just find ways round each other, like a big game of Chinese Checkers. They have bizarre double-decker buses here, with fronts hooked on to lorry cabs so that they slope sharply towards the rear. Some tongas are drawn by horses decorated with hennaed patterns. Camels plod along snootily pulling carts. Their coats are cut in zig-zag designs.

We never cease to be astonished by the number of large hump-backed cows with huge shapely horns, idling in the middle of the road, lurking round every corner chewing newspapers, cardboard boxes, or anything else they can get hold of. They loll around as if aware of their exalted status and haunting beauty. Though they spread disease, disrupt traffic and browse on crops desperately needed for human food, their slaughter is forbidden.

SACRED COW AND CALF

FORTUNE-TELLER AND HIS GREEN PARROT

India's 300 million cows are not actually worshipped as deities, and many of them are not especially well treated, but they are symbols of Shiva, the supreme god of creation and destruction, and as such are considered sacred and venerated by all Hindus. Many Hindus believe that a daily dose of a concoction of their five products – milk, urine, curd, butter and dung – will cleanse the body inside and out. Cows are essential to many aspects of Indians' lives – for transport and farming power and as milk and manure providers.

Chris has his fortune told by a green parrot. The little bird hops out of its cage and unhesitatingly selects an envelope from a pile. His keeper then

ROAD MENDERS AND SACRED COW

interprets the contents with the help of an almanac. A friendly bystander translates for Chris: 'You are alone from the age of 23. There are troubles within your family. You are distracted and cannot settle – because of the planets. Your parents cannot help you. Your gift is from the gods. You will try many things but from the New Year everything you try will fail. You will not find happiness with a woman. . . .' At this point the translator apologizes profusely: 'This is not me saying these things, it is only what he is telling me.' 'No, no, it is not me, it is the bird . . . but for only 5 rupees more I can help you with these problems. . . .'

We walk down to the dried-up Sabarmati River

bed through streets inches thick in dust and sand, and lined with shanty town and squalor. Donkeys and goats graze on the river bed while children fly kites and play cricket. We pass makeshift huts and washing lines, open sewer pipes and go-as-you-please toilet areas, a huge circus tent and vast expanses of drying dyed fabric. Surrounded by smoggy views of downtown city blocks and smoking factory chimneys, it is the quietest place we have found all day.

We eat a wonderful Gujarati *thali* dinner (the traditional all-you-can-eat vegetarian meal) and join the hubbub outside the Regal cinema showing 'For the first time . . . TARZAN'. The poster looks spectacular. It shows 'African' tribesmen with macho Indian moustaches and an Asian Tarzan. The heroine is struggling in the river with a rubber ring painted to look like a snake.

21st January – Palitana

The region known as Saurashtra is a large peninsula jutting into the Arabian Sea. It was never part of British India but survived as more than 200 princely states right up to Independence. The country people dress distinctively. The men look like Balkan shepherds in their white jodhpurs with baggy seats and drainpipe legs. Over these they wear short-waisted frilled white smock tops with silver necklaces and chains around the waist. With white turbans or knitted hats on their heads, they drape folded blankets and shawls across their shoulders. Huge gold earrings pierce the middle of their ears. The women wear embroidered backless halter tops with plain inserts covering their breasts.

Palitana lies at the foot of a large hill which is one of the holiest pilgrimage places for members of the Jain religion. Over lunch yesterday we met our first Jain, a fat businessman who is well acquainted with Hatton Garden but knows no other part of London. He is a Bombay diamond merchant who travels all over the world 'but you will never find anywhere a place such as this'. He is a strict Jain who won't harm a living creature. Not only is he a vegetarian but he also won't eat root vegetables like potatoes, onions and garlic, lest in the pulling of them a tiny creature may be harmed. He fasts every night from 7 p.m. till 8.15 a.m. He comes here on the same day every month to climb the hill and worship for the whole day. He fasts from the night before and walks up barefoot and clothed all in white. He is shadowed by a yes-man who echoes his every senti- ment and grins fanatically. They invite us to share a pot of tea with them and then pay for our lunch. We thank them, but no, they must thank us for giving them the opportunity to be so generous. 'We are very lovable people, very warm and loving. Whenever we come here we pay for other people's meals, even if the hotel is full. All the staff are grateful to me. My name is Prakesh, which means "light" in your country, Prakesh Shah.' Their room is next door to ours. Before going to sleep, Chris performs his nightly mosquito hunt. The thuds of this lengthy ritual must have kept the two Jains awake half the night praying for our souls and those of the unfortunate mosquitoes.

In the morning we walk through the town, past the post office which has a bees' nest on the door, to the base of the hill and the groups of walking-stick sellers and 'dooli-wallahs', who carry people up the 8000 steps on swinging seats hung from poles across the shoulders or in cane chairs on a platform. Many Jains dressed in white and carrying sticks are already making their way down. It's an hour and a sweaty, temple-throbbing half to the summit – Shatrunjaya, the 'Place of Victory', which is crowned by 863 temples, built over the last nine hundred years.

The all-white hilltop is an awesome conglomera- tion of stepped towers and little domes, topped with bird tables and adorned with red and white flags and streamers. There are an astonishing num- ber of people up here – sweepers, bearers, offering sellers, officials, temple guardians, labourers, priests and pilgrims. The hilltop is dedicated entirely to the gods and no-one is allowed to stay on the hill after dusk, so all these people must walk up and down to work every day. . . .

My photography permit only allows me to photograph the exteriors of the buildings. The tem- ple interiors are packed with images of the 24 Jain saints known as Tirthankars or 'finders of the path' (to total cosmic consciousness). They sit in Buddha poses but their facial expressions are very different. They have bright pop eyes, blobby and slightly elongated fingers and toes, a pointed nose and an eerie thin smile. They are glossy and sleek and look

SAURASHTRAN MEN WAITING AT AHMADABAD BUS STATION

rather amphibious. Two young Jain brothers who go to a Jesuit school in Bangalore explain some of the rituals and proceedings to us. The pilgrims chant their common mantra and adorn the statues with splashes of yellow sandalwood 'paint' and red roses, the only flowers Jains use. They must be placed with the right hand only. The worshippers make patterns on little stools and tables with offerings of rice, fruit and nuts. Favoured symbols are the moon and the swastika. The swastika design, the reverse of the Nazi emblem, is a bearer of good luck and is often painted on doorways and used in brand labels throughout India. To place offerings on some of the holiest altars, which are behind locked wooden screens, the pilgrims must change their garments for robes which will only be used for this purpose. Many of the monks wear cloth masks over the mouth to avoid any risk of accidentally swallowing an insect.

The entire hilltop is walled in. The tops of the walls are covered in the severest profusion of broken glass I have ever seen. So much for not wanting to harm a living thing! Coming down takes just as long as going up, with a few breaks to soothe our aching calves. At the bottom of the hill several new temples and a Jain museum are under construction, including 'the unique, vertical and horizontal circular temple without pillars'. Jains are obviously a rich community who buy indulgences with monuments to the gods (and themselves?). As if 863 temples on one hill aren't enough!

23rd January – Diu island

We are staying in a beautiful one-storey, whitewashed hotel with a large verandah, over-looking the channel to the mainland. The town, formerly Portuguese, has a very relaxed atmo-sphere, narrow leafy lanes and ornamented, brightly painted buildings. We find three big Catholic churches. One, adjoining a school, is still functioning, with masses in Portuguese and English. The pastel blue of the rococo facade is peeling. Another has been converted into a hospital and dispensary. The third contains a badminton court.

We breakfast on the verandah, watching the little ferries chug back and forth from the cubist village of Goghla. The fishing boats and large canoes stop above the submerged sandbanks in the middle of the channel. The fishermen appear to be walking on water as they spread out their nets. Below us young men wade up to their shoulders to net their catch. Groups of cheery women pass up and down with large bundles on their heads, washing and vege-tables and a large fish in a silver bowl. We shop for fruit in the market square and catch the bus to the beach at Nagoa, halfway down the island.

Nagoa beach is a beautiful crescent of fine sand backed by groves of coconut and branching palms. A collection of reed huts marks a small hippie col-ony. In a native village two bullocks turn a wheel connected to a much larger wooden wheel on

BULLOCKS TURNING A WATER WHEEL, DIU

which clay pots are bound with rope. The whole contraption is held together with wooden pegs and irrigates the surrounding fields. Cows and goats nestle in glades along the exotic leafy paths in the middle of the island. The tiny village of Fudam is dominated by the empty Church of Our Lady of Remedies – empty except for the elaborately carved wooden altarpiece, pulpit and fonts. The Virgin and Child look down with enlarged Hindu eyes and Our Lady has a red *bindi* on her forehead.

Just outside the walls of Diu town several cricket matches are in play. Down by the fishermen's huts the fishwives are hanging out row upon row of fish to dry. A little girl screams 'hippie, hippie' at us.

HANGING UP FISH TO DRY

A day travelling in Gujarat

The 8 o'clock bus from Diu skirts the northern tidal marsh and salt pans to the small fishing village of Vanakbara. To the amusement of the locals we must wade out with our bags and up the treacherous gangplank to board the ferry over to the mainland at Kodala. The women sit with their large bundles in the prow of the boat, forming a colourful triangle of brightly patterned cloths and dazzling jewellery. Their earlobes droop under the weight of large gold earrings. Several smaller rings are worn at the top of the ear, often joined by a chain to a large nose ring. A number of finger and toe rings, big silver anklets and bundles of dowry bracelets and armbands complete the display. Some women also have blue designs tattooed on to their arms, legs and necks. Their babies wear fierce black eye make-up. The men stick together at the rear.

At Kodala, which is just a handful of sleepy houses, we transfer to 'tempos' – large three-wheeled motorbikes with a couple of wooden benches across the back – for the 12-mile ride to Kodinar. The journey is horrendous. At first I sit on a metal rim at the back but it's so painful that I change to one of the wooden planks. We hang on for dear life as the bike picks up speed on an open stretch of bumpy road. We pick up more and more people who sit casually on the edge of the thing while we grip tightly. Our bodies are racked with tension and our bums ache. I count 17 of us, plus a mass of bags and luggage, including one woman who manages to breast-feed her baby in the middle of all this with absolute calm and dignity. In Kodinar we pay our 2 rupees fare and wobble up the hot dusty street to the bus station, aware that we are now back in India proper after a few days' respite in peaceful Diu.

In the small bus station we sit down and immedi-ately 30 or so people gather in front of us to stare. The cracks in the crowd only reveal more staring faces and we can feel the pressure of another 30 pairs of eyes on the backs of our heads. We don't know where to look! They don't let up until two men in handcuffs are led through the station.

When a bus pulls in the ensuing scenes are grotesque. Before it has stopped the door is forced open and men start clambering over each other to get on board. Bags and children are passed through the windows. After the initial surge the embarking hordes suffer a setback as the disembarking forces shove from within. Battle rages for a full ten minutes until the bell goes and the engine starts up. The bus pulls out with three people hanging out the door, half of their limbs inside the bus and the other half out. As it passes through the gate and on to the road the door swings shut and off it goes. One half expects to see heads and limbs bursting through the roof. We are left awaiting our bus in trepidation.

Laden down with our baggage, we are forced to let the young warrior caste fight it out first while we join the ranks of silent women and try to squeeze on when the bus is already full. We pass a group of four round faces painted on a wall. We have seen the same sign before but now realise it dates from an early seventies birth-control campaign, showing the happy two-child family. The landscape is arid, divided up by drystone walls and hedges of cacti with tiny pink flowers. The journey is very slow and uninteresting but not without incident. At one point we leave the road and cross a ditch and several fields before remounting the road only to hit a post, jamming the door and the bus halfway across a railway line. Panic-stricken passengers dive through the windows.

At the next stop we get out to have a cold drink and another crowd gathers round. How people stare at our watches! We are forever being asked for the time and how much our watches cost, when often the enquirer is wearing a much bigger and flashier watch of his own.

We have some fun with a group of schoolboys, who are amazed that we have neither gods nor wives. 'What is your religion?' is generally the second question we are asked on buses and trains. It comes after 'What is your country?' and before 'What is your good name?', 'What is your service?'

and 'How much do you earn?'. Hindus are so religious and so convinced that one must have a religion. It wouldn't matter in the least if we say we are Moslem or that we worship the sun, but to have no religion or to not believe in God arouses disdainful surprise.

It is the bumpiest ride yet along largely unpaved roads in virtual desert, with stops in tiny villages where men and boys clamber up the sides of the bus. All sorts of trade is done through the windows – nuts, biscuits, fruit, tea, large green coconuts with straws, cigarettes and *beedis* (leaf cigarettes) and *pan*. *Pan* is a sweet or spicy mix of ingredients pasted on to a leaf and chewed with betel nuts, which can be slightly intoxicating. The spitting out of the leftovers accounts for the red blotches spattered all over the place.

Chris is befriended by a man who speaks a little English and has the largest belly on the bus. He puts on Chris's straw hat and sits on his friend's lap so that Chris can sit down. He invites us to his house for dinner and to stay the night. He comes close to tears when we won't get off the bus with him. Meanwhile a young Moslem with several children

DESERT VILLAGE

BATHING GHATS AT DWARKA

and at least one wife in tow is giving me the eye. He smiles and wiggles his eyebrows at me and tries to get his friend to get me to look at him. Eventually we reach Porbandar, birthplace of Gandhi, a dusty town with cement and chemical factories and a smelly fishing harbour.

26th January – Porbandar and Dwarka

Today is Republic Day. We walk round looking in vain for festivities. Last night when all the dogs in town seemed particularly deranged by the full moon, howling in packs and picking fights with cows, we did witness one procession: a small group of pipe-players and drummers and a 'maharaja' type figure on a white pony were led by several black dancers in grass skirts. There are a number of Indianized Africans in this area, called Siddis, who form a separate caste of Harijans (untouchables). Our hotel room backs on to a huge cinema and we open the bathroom door to the roars of lions and the screams of people falling down wells.

We sit in a 'park' full of pigeons and cows till it's time to take the bus to Dwarka. In front of us a woman gives a holy man a massage, legs and back, then combs his long hair for him. Meanwhile a magnificent, thick-necked, black and brown bull with a huge hump lifts its tail and instantly a young girl runs forward and 'delivers' a healthy steaming 8lb turd with all the tenderness of a trained mid-wife. She slaps it into a basket and puts it on her little brother's head. He runs off, delighted with his swag, only to trip over a stone and deposit the load onto the dusty ground where it was headed in the first place.

Dwarka is one of the four holiest Hindu pilgrimage sites in India – Lord Krishna is said to have dipped his toe in the sea here. However it is remote and small, and remains calm and relaxed. We walk past a cattle fair on our way down to the bathing ghats which lie on an inlet from the sea. Up a long flight of steps, lined with souvenir sellers, stands the main Dwarkanath temple, with its five-storeyed tower topped by a huge triangular white flag billowing majestically in the sea breeze. The lesser shrines contain carved stone images elaborately dressed in flowing robes and decorated with coloured silver papers, jewels and armour. The main temple is packed with worshippers crowding

EVENING SCRUB

TEMPLES ON THE BEACH, DWARKA

to see the hallowed image inside. Men and women sit outside in separate groups chanting mantras.

By the sea there are many little shrines and cells for pilgrim sadhus. They huddle inside smoking and praying, or sit outside washing and bathing or meditating on the large sandy beach in the brilliant sunset. Long formations of flamingos cross the sky.

A line of naval gunboats patrols the horizon near the border with Pakistan. The full moon rises over Lord Krishna's temple.

30th January – Bhuj
Kutch is the westernmost part of India, separated from the peninsula that is Saurashtra by the Gulf of

DESERT FARMS IN THE RANN OF KUTCH

Kutch and from the Sind region of Pakistan by the Great Rann (desert) of Kutch.

Bhuj, the major town of Kutch, is an old walled city with a lively bazaar and a maze of narrow streets and alleyways with displays of tie-dyed, embroidered and mirrored fabrics and the occasional snake in a basket. One alley opens up into a grain market square full of decorated 'Public Carrier' lorries and camel carts. In the middle is a huge ornate oversubscribed pigeon tower. When they are startled into mass flight, the pigeons darken the sky as they sweep around like a dancer's veil. A huge crowd gathers round our café as Chris draws the square. Inevitably coffee gets spilt all over the sketchbook. The kind café owner mops up Chris's book lovingly and dries it in his oven. He gives us more coffee on the house and shoos away the crowd.

The old city walls surround a large 'lake' which is really a water tank fed by streams and rainwater. Throughout the subcontinent these tanks provide water for irrigation and drinking and are used as a

ANOINTING A SHRINE

place to water livestock and wash clothes. The Kutch museum has three large crocodile specimens caught in this tank, but all we see are large terrapins. The women wash their clothes in the traditional fashion by beating them against stones. They then lay out the colourful cotton saris and white men's dhotis in abstract patterns on the sandy earth to dry. While drawing this scene we are mobbed by a gang of excitable schoolchildren who follow us around chanting 'Eur-o-pean, Eur-o-pean!'.

We take a tonga – horse and cart – from Mandvi to the Vijayvilas Palace, the former winter residence of the last 'King of Kutch'. He spent the rest of the year in London. We go past the new wind pumps on the beach – an electric power scheme funded by the guru Bhagwan Rajneesh and soon to be opened by 'Mr India', Rajiv Gandhi. Turning idly in the breeze, they resemble aeroplane propellors on sticks. The Palace is a 1920s Anglo-Moghul residence with cool marble floors and dull English furniture. It has no character and is devoid of decorative craftsmanship in traditional materials like wood and fabrics. From the rooftop we catch our last glimpse of the sea over the tops of the

surrounding coconut plantations. Rajneesh and his red-dressed followers wanted to buy this residence too but the locals objected.

Back in Bhuj, we meet up with our new friend Kantilal in the little tea shop near the Shri Narayan temple, a large rainbow-painted building with the most beautiful shrines we have yet seen. Kantilal brings his friend, Mr Khatri – a Moslem who works in the Bank of India branch in the old palace. They both have many interests and hobbies – birdwatching clubs, photography (they have their own enlargers and darkrooms), stamp collecting, astrology, Indian philosophy and mysticism . . . and meeting foreigners in Bhuj. They are both very friendly. They take us to see some of their artist friends and talk a lot about the traditional village life in the Banni region nearby. When we are leaving they make a polite request to be sent something special from England. Kantilal asks for a book on 'monochrome darkroom techniques' and Mr Khatri would like a picture book about 'your Princess Diana'.

OPPOSITE: FARMER AND STORKS

Rajasthan

3rd February – Mount Abu

AT LAST WE ARRIVE in Rajasthan, the fabled 'Land of the Kings'. Spread out along a 4000-foot-high plateau just over the Gujarati border is Mt Abu, Rajasthan's only hill station. An hour-long dawn ascent by jeep gives spectacular views of a sea of mist covering the plains below, pierced by dark sails of rock. The plateau is very rugged with large hills and black boulders softened by palm trees and exotic vegetation. A popular holiday resort with honeymooners, it is packed with hotels, cafés and souvenir shops. It is

GREEN FIELD IN THE THAR DESERT

DUDH-WALLAHS BY NAKKI LAKE

decidedly off-season so they are all competing desperately for trade: 'YES you turn right for CHACHA Museum', 'Shopping in Chacha Museum is as enjoyable as boating on Nakki Lake'. The artificial Nakki Lake boasts 'romantic' punt rides. An intermittent procession of 'dudh-wallahs' appears up a stepped path coming from who-knows-where with silver milk churns on their heads. A brown mongoose pops in and out of his hole by the lake.

In the evening we walk to Sunset Point to look out over the plains below. A dry river bed meanders across the parched landscape. Ridges of purple are shrouded in mist and the sunset sky is a fusion of rainbow colours.

BHIL WOMEN

BHIL WOMEN FETCHING WATER

5th February – Udaipur

The buses in Rajasthan are more crowded than ever, often with an additional 'top deck' of passengers sitting on all the baggage. However, the 'luxury, non-stop' bus ride from Mt Abu is exhilarating not just for the comfort, but because of the magnificent traditional dress of the locals (mainly Bhils in this region). Whether labouring at roadworks, on building sites, in the fields or out collecting firewood, the women wear very full long skirts called *ghagras*, sometimes using as much as 20 yards of material, with long embroidered bodices and veils over their heads which reach down to the hem of the skirt. All in brilliant patterns and hues of pinks and reds, these costumes are worn with extravagant dowry jewellery – multiple earrings attached to a large silver nose ring, silver anklets, toe rings and armfuls of bracelets and ivory armbands up to their shoulders. Rajasthani men are extremely tall and good-looking with fine facial features and fierce 'soup-strainer' moustaches. They wear a dhoti wrapped tightly around the legs, a tunic buttoned up the front and a brightly dyed turban which identifies their caste and community. Plain, block-printed or tie-dyed, the colour and pattern of the enormously long piece of turban fabric and the intricate way in which it is wrapped vary from region to region. As we travelled through Rajasthan we found the length of skirt and style of chunky jewellery also changed frequently.

Udaipur is the largest and busiest town we have been in for some time and at first we are overwhelmed by all it has to offer. It is also the most romantic. The peaceful shore of Lake Pichola offers a splendid panorama of the town. A short stretch of water separates us from a small island occupied by the Lake Palace Hotel. A former maharaja's residence, it featured in the James Bond film *Octopussy*. Many of the locals talk about the time when Roger Moore was here. His autographed photo graces several tea-shop walls and it seems everybody has a brother or cousin who was involved in the film.

Outside the grounds of the City Palace we come across a demonstration by staff of the Lake Palace Hotel, who are on hunger strike over conditions and pay and the management's contempt for their union. Beneath a fiery red sky, the blue hills rimmed by pink remind us of wild Connemara. A travelling musician with a two-stringed fiddle and bells on his bow plays and sings to the women for 10 or 20 paise as they sit on their doorsteps.

Many houses have paintings of elephants and tigers round their doorways, done at the time of marriage ceremonies. Frescos painted by the artisan castes on the walls of Rajput houses depict family heroes and serve to identify the superior caste of the homeowner. Throughout the old area by the lake there are overhanging balconies with little shuttered openings and Moslem arches creating a look of fading grandeur. Bad sanitation and poor sewage disposal gives much of the town a very unpleasant stench!

The folk-craft museum is a strange-shaped building with an intriguing collection of Rajasthani folklore trappings. The customs and costumes are all well explained, and there are sections on *menhadi* (the patterned hennaing of women's hands and feet practised at festivals and marriage ceremonies) and the symbolism of traditional designs finger-painted on mud houses. The curator himself puts on a lively and humorous puppet show every hour.

9th February – Pushkar

It is dark when we pull into Ajmer station, very dark. The station district is having an electricity blackout. The train stops one track away from the moving cigarette butts and candle-lit stalls on the busy platform. I step softly off the train into something unspeakable. We climb onto the platform and inch our way over the stepbridge and through the crowds of travellers, soldiers and bundles of baggage out to the street. We ignore all the hotel touts who tell us the buses to Pushkar have finished till the morning. When the bus comes there's an almighty struggle to get on, but our experience is beginning to tell and despite our luggage not only do we get on but we get seats. The driver has trouble finding first gear and it takes three people to wrestle the lever into submission. The 7-mile trip up a hill and down the other side takes a full hour.

The small town clings to the side of a beautiful holy lake in which only brahmins, the top caste, can bathe. The shore is packed with temples and bathing ghats where footwear and photography are vociferously prohibited. Every November at the full moon of Kartik Poornima the tiny population is

WOMEN WASHING AT THE LAKE

swamped by about half a million visitors, on two legs and four, for the legendary cattle fair, one of India's biggest and most spectacular festivals. In between times it is a laid-back travellers' town full of hippie souvenir shops and secondhand English paperback stalls.

Beyond the town small groups of straw huts in deadwood corrals nestle in the sand dunes which signal the start of the desert. Ominous dark clouds crash into each other and the rain pelts down. We find a shelter with a panoramic view of the lake and watch the ensuing hail storm, torrential rain and violent thunder and lightning. It eases after an hour and the surrounding hilltops re-emerge. The streets are flooded. There are pools everywhere and the animals look half-drowned. We drink a comforting hot chocolate in a lakeside café listening to Lou Reed singing about Berlin. The washing we left out to dry has been beaten into the ground and is now dirtier than ever.

12th–16th February – Jaisalmer

Jodhpur railway station is covered with sleeping and squatting forms. Outside a line of chairs faces a row of mirrors on the wall. The barbers complete their early morning grooming routine with a quick shave under the armpits. A cheeky macaque monkey steals a bundle of chappatis from a breakfasting family.

The 8 a.m. Jodhpur–Jaisalmer 'express' is pulled by a magnificent steam locomotive with a silver star on its pointed nose. Our carriage is overrun with people and their belongings, in particular a tone-deaf pipe-player and his entourage of two wives and seven scabby kids. As the children become increasingly bored the carriage gets noisier and dirtier, and I'm not the only one to give them a clip round the ear. We become unbearably uncomfort-able after only a few hours of sitting on the flat wooden seats. The prospect of ten hours of this physical discomfort and aural torture is pushed to the limits when the piper produces a snake from a basket and starts passing it round the confined compartment. The bars on the window prevent Chris from hurling himself to certain death and he spends the rest of the journey in a sweat by the open train door on a heap of cabbages.

Weaver birds' nests hang from bare shrubs and birds of prey circle overhead. In a sleepy station we stop next to a huge banyan tree full of peacocks jumping noisily from branch to branch. A man in a bright yellow turban points to his house and invites us to stay with him.

At first there are yellow patches of earth that suggest hay or crops in the short rainy season. Then the red sandstone scrubland gives way to barren desert, empty except for darting gazelle and army tank units and encampments. At Ramdeora there is a local festival in progress to honour a bearded saint who rides a white horse.

OPPOSITE: THIEVING MONKEYS AT THE RAILWAY STATION

THE ROYAL PALACE AT JAISALMER

The small walled town of Jaisalmer sits in the middle of the vast Thar Desert. The whole town is built of yellow sandstone and from the humblest shop to the Royal Palace and the temples it glows with the same golden colour. The tangled maze of narrow streets and alleys contains magnificent merchants' houses, called *havelis*, decorated with exquisite stone carvings. The little desert 'island' of Jaisalmer has been off the beaten track since the camel trains ceased plying the Silk Route bringing trade from distant Samarkand and Bukhara. It is back on the map now because of its strategic importance near the sensitive Pakistan border, which has brought paved roads, trains, electricity

THAR DESERT VILLAGE

FRUIT AND VEGETABLE STREET-MARKET IN JAISALMER

and with them a new money-spinner – tourism.

Jaisalmer is very calm and relaxed, very definitely a holiday town, with tour groups of pampered, old Americans and Germans being led around its exotic attractions on camels. The moonlit crenellated medieval ramparts with their starry backdrop are like a fantastic opera set from the *Tales of a Thousand and One Nights* – the most romantic sight we've seen!

We breakfast in a café, listening to Beatles tapes. It is fascinating to watch the continuous activity in the streetside foodstalls and restaurants, from dawn till late at night. The clay ovens and gas burners are right on the street. Young boys are busy making and serving tea, chopping wood, podding peas, preparing panloads of vegetables, crushing spices, mixing bread-doughs. . . . All day long the process continues, up to the evening climax when the chappatis are rolled, slapped around between the palms and stuck to the inside roof of the oven. The *puris* are deep fried. The sticky sweets which have been pounded into an orange paste earlier in the day are piped into hot fat. Vast, saucer-shaped iron pans full of milk are heated up. By one oildrum fire we can just make out a dark aboriginal-looking man, poking at the ashes and stoking the flames.

On one edge of town is a group of simply decorated mud and straw huts. These are the homes of the camel drivers. Every tourist who visits Jaisalmer goes on a camel safari, sleeping under the desert stars, eating with the camel drivers, visiting desert villages, experiencing the vast emptiness and getting to know yourself . . . and your camel!

A group of these full-mustachioed, noble-faced men call us over and explain there is a marriage feast in progress. They have just eaten an enormous mutton curry. All the women are in their most colourful garb and heavily ornamented. They show

us inside one small, dark hut where the bride is having *menhadi* designs painted on to her hands and feet. The celebrations will last for many days in the two villages of the bride and groom. A friend of theirs, whom they describe as a smuggler for our benefit, is dressed like a pantomime genie in a sparkling tunic with jewels in his turban. He carries a pike and a sword, but his most magnificent attribute is his twisted moustache which curls round and round on each of his cheeks, kept in place by a cord passing from his ears under his nose. We are told that when straightened out, each side of his 'tache is a yard long.

Back in the town we pass another ceremony. Outside a house in mourning, two male members of the family are having their heads shaved while groups of women wearing dark blue or maroon weep and wail loudly.

A young boy from Barmer, another Thar Desert town, talks to us excitedly. He asks us, 'Why are you so thin when your country is not poor?'

The cows in this town have a tendency to swing their heads in our direction as we pass. At first we think it is coincidental but as it becomes more

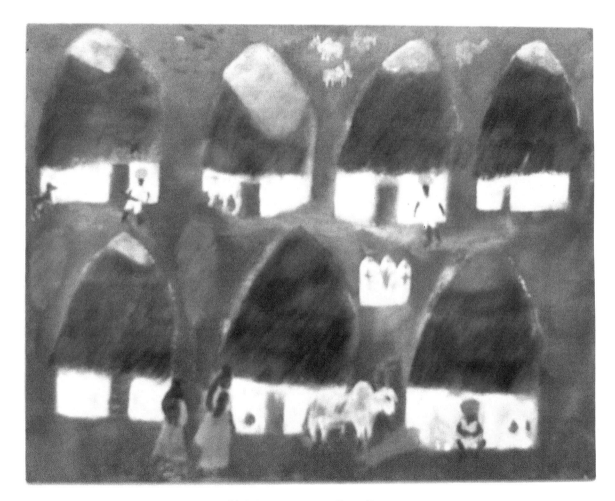

MUD HOUSES IN THE THAR DESERT

blatant and aggressive and their horns catch in our clothes and graze our skins we give them a wider berth (Jaisalmer – 'Pamplona of the East').

Next day, in a fit of bravado, Chris gets his hair cut for 5 rupees, and very nice it is too. Encouraged by this we stick our necks out even further and hire bicycles for the afternoon. We gingerly wheel them right out of town and tensely cycle out 5 miles in search of a little oasis called Bada Bagh. I am terrified and stop any time there is anything in sight moving faster than a grazing camel. Just outside Jaisalmer at 'Sunset Point' are a collection of brahmin mausoleums with a fantastic view of the double-walled town in the orange light. Several busloads of tourists are being entertained by squeaky musicians and costumed girls dancing like disco puppets. It is a comical sight.

20th February – Jaipur

The old walled Rajasthan capital of Jaipur is known as the 'pink city' because of the orange-pink sandstone from which all its buildings are constructed. It is laid out in neat rectangles formed by broad, busy avenues. Its long facades and terracotta turrets

STREET IN JAIPUR

glow warmly and magically in the evening light.

In the heart of the Old City, by the City Palace, saris dyed bright yellow with red borders and large red circles are drying in the sun. Across from the Palace is the Jantar Mantar, the 18th-century Royal Observatory built by the great warrior-astronomer and founder of the city, Maharaja Jai Singh II. The Observatory today is a fascinating and impressive collection of huge instruments designed to measure latitude and longitude and track the movements of the sun, the planets and the stars. The precision on such a large scale (the sundial is 100 ft high) is breathtaking and the surreal ensemble makes a delightfully sublime sculpture garden.

The famous Hawa Mahal ('Palace of Winds') is a five-storeyed pink facade of delicately honey-combed bay 'windows' built to allow the ladies of the Royal Household to observe the streetlife and processions below. From the top are excellent views over the city to the nearby hills. As the visitors leave at closing time, the palace is re-occupied by families of brown, short-tailed, pink-faced rhesus macaque monkeys. The pavement outside is a gathering place for beggars and cripples.

A few miles outside Jaipur, on a hillside over-looking a lake, sits the fortress-palace and former Rajput capital of Amber. We are feeling a little fort drunk from our tour of Rajasthan. While helping to create the exotic and romantic atmosphere of Rajasthan, they serve as a clear reminder of the state's warlike past. The 'Majestic Fort' of Jodhpur is the most formidable in Rajasthan, perched on a rock which rises sheer out of the blue-painted houses of the brahmins. The 15 handprints by its final entrance gates are the suttee marks of widows of Maharaja Man Singh, who threw themselves upon his funeral pyre in 1843. The history of the hilltop fortress of Chittorgarh is gruesomely 'romantic'. Three times the fort was overwhelmed by enemies. On each occasion all the men donned the orange robes of martyrdom and rode out to certain death, leaving their women and children behind to perish in a huge funeral pyre in the ritual suicide known as *jauhar*. The bravery and sense of honour of the Rajput warriors is legendary and dictated events in this region for a thousand years.

The Northern Plains

24th February – Agra

WE TAKE A trishaw to India's most famous monument, the Taj Mahal. The strength in the legs of our young excited driver doesn't match his enthusiasm and we feel a surge of guilt. It's a long hard slog to earn a meagre 3 rupees. On a steep slope he gets off and starts to push, so we climb down and join him.

An endless flow of Indian and foreign tourists stroll up and down the formal gardens and fountain

OPPOSITE: OLD DELHI RAILWAY STATION

approach. Tiny figures move around the white marble base of the Mahal. We are amused by the 'professional' photographers positioning their clients. Their customers are very obedient and adopt the stiff serious postures of their forebears.

It's dark inside the Taj. Guides shine torches against the inlaid walls and tombs to highlight the intricate patterns and the translucent quality of the white marble. The Taj, flanked by twin red sandstone mosques, is built on an enormous marble platform overlooking the Yamuna River. Across the river, reed fences shelter patches of watermelons growing on the sandbanks and water buffaloes slouch in the shallows. Upstream looms the imposing silhouette of the Red Fort, where Shah Jahan, who built the Taj in memory of his favourite wife, was imprisoned by his son Aurangzeb.

Along the river bank cotton-wrapped corpses smoulder on cremation ghats. We cross the Yamuna by the arched iron railway bridge and look down on rows of 'dhobi-wallahs' and their patchwork of drying washing. On through green wheat

OPPOSITE: THE TAJ MAHAL

fields and a small village to the riverbank facing the Taj. By now we have attracted 16 young disciples, all demanding pens, rupees, watches, chocolate and attention. In between requests they hawk and spit noisily. We have to shout loudly in their faces and walk further down the bank to escape them.

The sun goes down behind the fort. The full moon is already high in the sky. Blasts of heat rise from the earth as we retrace our steps through the moonlit fields. The blurred form of a small boat glides softly past a mouse-coloured cow munching on roots at the water's edge.

Fatehpur Sikri
The 25-mile bus ride to Fatehpur Sikri provides entertainment in the form of travelling salesmen demonstrating their wares, a succession of horrific road accidents, a couple of dancing bears and packs of shabby vultures. The village is infested with flies. It seethes with their fat black shapes, crawling over everyone and everything.

The deserted capital of the Emperor Akbar is a perfectly preserved 16th-century Moghul city abandoned after only 16 years because of difficulties with the water supply. At the entrance gate is a huge mosque, said to be a copy of that in Mecca. Inside the fort it is calm and quiet. The red sandstone palaces are square and chunky rather than arched and delicate. They are built to a very open design and appear somewhat whimsical and impractical. The ghost town would seem more impressive if it wasn't 'haunted' by gangs of swanky young Indians clacking around in their cuban heels and giggling hysterically.

We are fortunate to find a secluded rooftop overlooking a busy excavation site. The colourful scene is a typical Indian worksite, incredibly labour-intensive and inefficient. Men are pickaxeing the sandy earth and breaking up the larger stones while teams of women form a continuous procession with small baskets on their heads half-filled with earth or a rock. They walk to a mound 30 yards away, empty their load and walk slowly back for more. Roadside gangs often utilize two workers to each spade. One pushes the blade down, the other helps to lift it out by pulling on a string attached to the shovel. On city building sites babies and small children play in makeshift open-air 'crèches'

beneath the rickety towers of bamboo scaffolding.

At the archaeological site a man in a suit consults a plan and supervises the dig. A large area is divided up into small squares by white stones. The squares contain shards of pottery which if stuck together would be identical to the beautiful traditional round-bottomed pots on sale in the market down the road. An old woman sits by a basin of water washing the finds. The workers seem rather bemused by the whole performance.

28th February – Delhi

New Delhi is not like the rest of India. The roads and pavements are broad. The traffic is more or less under control and stops at traffic lights and junctions. There are few cows, and no pigs, buffaloes or camels in the streets, little dust, and no chillies for breakfast. There are public toilets, good bookshops to browse in, air-conditioned fast-food restaurants and underground shopping centres (to combat the deadly heat of summer).

The great circle of Connaught Place is the heart

OPPOSITE: ARCHAEOLOGICAL DIG AT FATEHPUR SIKRI

of New Delhi. We sit in its grassy centre to read our letters from home, oblivious to all offers of food and drink, massages, shoeshines, earcleans, drugs and black-market deals.

North of Connaught Place an invisible barrier separates spacious, relaxed, sophisticated New Delhi from chaotic, noisy, crowded, dirty, pungent Old Delhi. The transition is so immediate and complete it is startling. New Delhi is chic and aloof. Old Delhi is full of life, ancient, grubby and well worn, where privacy and peace have no place.

Outside the Jami Masjid, India's largest mosque, pilgrims camp on the balding grass, their goats skipping about happily. Men wash their bodies and clothes publicly with a hosepipe. Everywhere food is being prepared, cooked and sold. Beggars sit solemnly at the food of the steps below the mosque's massive courtyard. Women in purdah scurry by, revealing flashes of colour beneath their black enveloping burkas. The taped prayers from the loudspeakers are deafening and distorted. I am given a length of checked cloth to cover my bare

OPPOSITE: NEW DELHI TRAFFIC

legs. We skulk around in the shade, avoiding the scorching flagstones which burn our feet, then climb to the top of a minaret to enjoy the slight breeze and a view over Delhi's rooftops. We are asked to leave before the 5 o'clock call to prayer.

The gardens and pavilions of the Red Fort are a haven of peace and calm after the frantic streets of Old Delhi. We sit next to a tethered white cow and a friendly hoopoe. The cow is led off to mow the lawns, another example of Indian labour inefficiency. The cow is harnessed to the front of the mower and is led by an attendant. A second assistant steers the mower from the rear.

There's a power cut as we walk through the narrow bazaar streets, but life carries on by candlelight. Gangs of skilled labourers sit on street corners, their tool bags beside them, waiting for work. Porters transport heavy loads of paper and other goods on their heads from delivery vehicles in the streets to their alleyway destinations. Two interminable lines of cycle rickshaws snake up and down the roads hissing at anyone who gets in their way. A large group of men squat outside a café eating their dinners off leaf plates. They perch three

STREET BATH

BATHING IN THE GANGES AT VARANASI

deep in the road facing the kitchen, backs to the traffic and fumes. It is humid and the streets are packed. People yell hello and want to chat. Mosques shimmer on every corner. Everybody is working in the semi-darkness until suddenly the lights come back on. The difference is astonishing. We're back in the 20th century – well sort of.

2nd March – Varanasi

Every devout Hindu yearns to visit Varanasi at least once. Sacred texts say that if a Hindu dies in this holy city and his ashes are scattered on the River Ganges, his soul will be released from rebirth and will be transported immediately to Lord Shiva's side in his Himalayan paradise.

PUJA AT THE BATHING GHATS

By 6.30 the sun is up and the river (which has 108 sacred titles) is crowded with large boats full of tour groups watching the city come alive in the magical first light. Dawn is a ritual prayer time for Hindus when many devotees perform puja. They stand in the water, make their offerings, immerse themselves and drink some of the holy water before going back up to the temples for morning prayer.

The mighty Ganga is broad. The opposite shore is only a distant sandbank. The city side is lined with over a hundred bathing ghats on great stepped embankments. As the day warms up the activity increases. The washerwomen beat their clothes clean and stretch them out to dry on the dusty

FISHERMEN

banks. Old bearded men meditate in twisted yoga positions. Others wade in to soap and wash their water buffaloes. Several inflated dog carcasses with crows pecking at them float past, followed by a decidedly human-looking rib-cage. Chris spots some of the freshwater dolphins we are told inhabit the river. Some of the bathing areas are like men's clubs, where the young and not-so-young parade around showing off their athletic bodies and engaging in body-building and fitness exercises. These are worshippers of the monkey god Hanuman, source of strength. But this is the city of Shiva, in whose matted hair (the Himalayas) lives the goddess Ganga. Each ghat has several Shiva shrines. The lingams (stone phalluses representing Shiva's creative role) and images of the bull Nandi (Shiva's mount) are daubed in oil, vermilion paste, jasmine blossoms and hibiscus flowers.

At the main burning ghat a smouldering fire is being poked about next to a queue of wrapped-up corpses. Male relatives and friends bring the shrouded bodies on litters and immerse them in the

OPPOSITE: DOWN BY THE TANK

Ganges. When dry they are placed on the pyres with offerings of sandalwood, camphor and ghee. Strict religious custom requires that the eldest son initiates all the rituals, because only his performance of the funeral rites is thought to ensure the successful release of the soul from earthly bondage. He fulfils this duty by bursting the flaming corpse's skull with a rod. Children are still innocent and do not need the purifying flames: their bound bodies are tied to stones and cast into the middle of Ganga Ma. Stacks of firewood are piled up behind scales for weighing and pricing the amount used per corpse – only wealthy families can afford enough timber to ensure a total cremation. A little way downstream a few salvage 'experts' are panning for gold and silver . . . from teeth and jewellery.

Pilgrims shelter from the intense sun under large wicker and cloth umbrellas. Some have had their body and clothes completely tattooed with the Sanskrit words 'Rama, Rama, Rama'. (Rama, like Krishna and Buddha, is one of the incarnations of the god Vishnu.) Beautiful dhows with patched sails move almost imperceptibly upstream near the opposite bank. Boatloads of mourners in white ferry to and from the burning ghats, delivering bodies and scattering ashes. Large stretches of the bank stink. There is no sewage treatment plant in Varanasi and all the sewage, along with everything else, ends up in the mighty Ganga.

Varanasi (Benares under the Raj) is famed throughout India for the quality of its silk brocades and saris. In the weaving district every dark little room is completely filled by a loom with a complex web of silk threads and stacks of punched cards. The old town is a maze of dark alleys beneath the towering old houses. The paths are barely wide enough for two people to pass, let alone the large-horned ownerless cows and bicycles that steam down the dirty passages and force us to take to the elevated doorsteps on either side. There are shops and small traders everywhere. We are overwhelmed! How on earth do they get their stocks in and out of their premises every day?

We escape from the labyrinth into filthy streets with channels of stagnant water full of large dead frogs. Some of the women are eerily clad in full flowery purdah, elasticated around the forehead and with gauze in the tiny round eyeholes. Large groups of orange-robed sadhus and pilgrims crowd the bare rooms of the numerous lodges.

Darkness falls. Down by the river children sell leaf boats to sail down the river. They are stitched together with twigs and hold bits of marigolds, rose petals and a dab of camphor with a wick. Storytellers sing romantic tales from the Hindu epic the *Ramayana*. Boatmen tout for rides. 'This is the best time' – a familiar phrase – 'the best time to see the burning ghats.' We can see the flames reflected a little downstream on the still, sleeping river. Butterlamps glow on the other ghats, suspended from tall, curved bamboo poles.

Clouds of thick dust hang in the sultry night air. The dry fumes of chillies catch our breath and make us cough repeatedly. The streets are teeming with bicycles and rickshaws and people. The rickshaw bells of Varanasi sound particularly musical. We walk past a magnificent curled-up sleeping black cow, a cute little brown donkey and a half-naked corpse lying unattended in the street. Always there is the potential to switch from relaxed ease and happiness in one's surroundings to instant paranoia and anxiety. Groups of armed and helmeted

TRAFFIC

soldiers are patrolling the streets. Recent Hindu-Moslem conflict resulted in curfews being imposed (an everyday occurrence somewhere or other in the country). We see other groups, like vigilantes, armed with sticks and lathis. The heavy atmosphere is deflated when one tall mustachioed officer shouts to us: 'Hello, my dears. How are you this evening?'

From Delhi to Darjeeling

As we walk through the claustrophobic second-class entrance, climbing over and between sitting and sleeping bodies, bags and packages, we almost panic – can four days in comfortable New Delhi really have softened us up that much? Old Delhi railway station on a Friday night is like a disturbed termites' nest – the numerous platforms and stairways are awash in a sea of surging white cotton homespun. All life is here, soldiers and sadhus, cows and corpses. Passers-by place coins and notes on a shrouded body on its way to an auspicious cremation at Varanasi. Alongside sits the widow in white, praying silently in a miraculous sanctuary of solitude she has created around herself, oblivious to the mayhem and impending stampede. Our names on the reservations list are virtually unrecognizable, having been 'translated' into Hindi, and then back again for our benefit.

'*Chai . . . chai . . . garumi chai . . .*' chorus the penetrating calls of the tea-wallahs for the umpteenth time in the night, competing with the insistent strain of a crying child and a carriage full of virtuoso rhythmic snorers. 'Indian music, strange to foreigners, is purely melodic and makes no use of the principle of harmony,' I remember reading somewhere.

We wake up to a new landscape, close to Lucknow in central Uttar Pradesh. It is astonishingly flat and very cultivated. Teams of bullocks plough the pink earth between fields of green millet and wheat and small crops of white poppies. Herons meditate, standing on one leg, in the blue and yellow flowers; goats are herded out to graze; yellow horses and spotted cows seek the umbrella shade of the huge-leaved banana trees. The tiled roofs of the village houses lie clustered in dark groves pierced by the distinctive white lotus-flower pinnacles of the Hindu temples. The mud walls are alive with the frescos of gods, men and animals, executed in yellows, ochres and umbers. Mounds of dung buns are attractively stacked by the outhouses, which are ornamented with elaborate patterns etched into the drying mud by the skilful fingers of a people alive to beauty.

Buffaloes wallow in marshy ground, which merges into expanses of shallow water edged by patches of bright colours where the washerwomen are hard at work. Men and women weave back and forth gracefully through the thick damp warmth, balancing huge sheaves of straw and bundles of wood on their heads.

Progress is slow and we make many stops. On

OPPOSITE: VILLAGE IN BIHAR

Barabanki station platform a young boy performs acrobatics and contortions. Several singing beggars work the carriages between stops. A proudly chanted tongue-twisting rhythmic litany with foot-stamping accompaniment advances tantalizingly slowly along the carriage. It heralds the arrival of a small mustachioed man selling nuts in conical paper packets arranged in a fan shape on a box strapped to his chest. One-third of India's people live in the broad, fertile Gangetic plain, one of the world's most densely populated areas. Once covered by water, it is still so level that all the way from Delhi to the Bay of Bengal, some 1200 miles, it drops only 660 feet.

Time passes much more slowly after dark. One hour after leaving Varanasi Junction our narrow-gauge steam train is still sitting in Varanasi City station. It's a long night and I unpack half of my bag to try and cushion my aching bones on the tortuous wooden bunk.

Dawn reveals a steamy landscape of paddy field, maize and sub-tropical vegetation. We are by now

OPPOSITE: PADDY FIELDS IN BIHAR

accustomed if not immune to the early morning parade of squatting bare bottoms – it's less fun than judging a Butlin's knobbly knees contest! The second act of the day is washing. As we pull into Bachwara station every pump, tap and hosepipe is busily employed washing lithe, naked torsos. Mobile food stalls are serving curried breakfasts on leaf plates stitched together with twigs. Noisy vendors tout their wares up and down the platform from big baskets and large trays carried on their heads: chappatis, samosas, poppadoms, soft drinks, oranges, slices of coconut, little *neem* branches (bitter-tasting twigs that serve as toothbrushes). The strong sweet *chai* is now sold in small disposable clay cups which we find difficult to throw out the window like everyone else.

On into Bihar, one of the poorest and most backward states in India. We pass by villages of reed houses with straw roofs and everywhere shrines and temples and humped cows. The train chugs on past grids of rice paddies, thickets of bamboo, rows of palms, huge pipal trees and strange, bare trees with large red flowers and pyramid-shaped trunks. Mountains of sugar cane are being cut and stacked onto bullock carts and rail freight wagons, lending a sweet smell to the already sultry atmosphere. Reed-covered boats rest on the deep blue lakes which pit the landscape, their fishing nets spread out in the shallows. Buffaloes wallow up to their noses in water, while the elephants bathe more playfully. Fried fish is on sale at the stations where poor family groups sit around waiting for who-knows-what. For the first time we see children with distended bellies. A small boy, tears streaming down his face, stands by our window, '*Das paise, babu . . . das paise, babu . . .* OK, *paisa baba. . . .*' Another child leads a blind beggarwoman from 'patron' to 'patron'. There are many beggars: 'Sahib, baksheesh, sahib. . .', 'Oh, *babu. . . .*'

All day long the scenery is exquisite, so calm and flat. Cyclists trace the mud banks of endless paddies. In the distance women with large bundles on their heads look like walking trees. Shiva's trident tops a beautiful white temple with a relief of a local 'saint' being torn apart by two leopards. The farmers favour a particularly vibrant shade of blue fabric in this region. The setting sun illuminates the waterlogged fields with a brilliant orange light,

which glistens off the wet hides of the water buffaloes being ridden home by the village boys. Night falls quickly and fireflies flicker by the open window, fleeing from the jackals which howl through the warm black night.

At 1 a.m. we alight at Siliguri station in West Bengal. A young army medic, a kind and gentle man who has shared his home-made food with us all the way from Varanasi, lies cocooned in his thick green issue sleeping bag, snoring softly. It is two and a half days since he left his wife and children in Poona and he must sit on this train another 36 hours to reach his destination in Nagaland by the tempestuous Burmese border.

The Himalayan foothills appear through the mist as we wait for the 7 o'clock 'toy' train. At 9 o'clock the tiny blue engine pulls in with its tiny first-class carriage, tiny second-class carriage and tiny goods wagon in tow – already overcrowded. More than 50 of us are squeezed into a carriage made for 32 midgets, but the journey is fun. The little train chugs along by the side of the road, criss-crossing it and stopping cars at some of the 132 unmanned level crossings, continuing upwards through very

SAINT WITH LEOPARDS TEMPLE, BIHAR

DALSING SARAI IN BIHAR

tall woods, past weatherboard houses raised on bricks or wooden stilts. The locals look oriental and are very short (a mix of Bengalis, Nepalis and Tibetan refugees) – is this the same country?

After a couple of hours, train lunches are passed through the windows at one of the little stations en route. Up and up we go, completing four loops and five switchbacks with wonderful views of the valleys and plains below. After four hours we reach Kurseong, perched atop the steep sloping hills. Thin blue ribbons of smoke rise from cooking-fires, hawks circle lazily overhead and we get our own seats. The train whistles its way right up the main street past the open shop-fronts. Children play at jumping on and off the slow-moving carriages on their way home from school.

By now we are in an exhausted daze. The breeze billowing through faded prayer flags tied to tall bamboo masts carries the hand block printed prayers up to the Buddhist gods. The golden pagoda monastery roofs shine out against the now cloudy sky. Circling the final loop our goal is revealed – the Victorian hill-station of Darjeeling ('Place of Thunderbolts'). The buildings are stacked on top of each other in an incredible variety of architectural styles, from British stone suburban semi-detached to Tibetan wooden simplicity, and spread across several hillsides. Below the last line of houses slope the terraces of the Happy Valley Tea Plantation. We are 7000 ft up and it's now very cold. Distant hills and ridges are shrouded in cloud and the mighty Himalayan peaks beyond might as well not be there.

Darjeeling and Nepal

8th March – Darjeeling

THE LOWER SLOPES of the town belong to the Nepalese, originally recruited by the British to work the tea plantations in the mid-19th century. Picturesque wooden shacks cling to the steep hillside almost on top of each other. Nepali men bear heavy loads of coal, firewood and grain in wicker baskets on their backs, with a strap around their foreheads. Lighter loads are carried in smaller baskets on poles. In the bazaar, next to the 'Licensed Bhang-Ganja Store', are coal and wood merchants who chop wood and break coal

BUDDHIST MONKS AND TIBETANS SPINNING PRAYER WHEELS

endlessly. They weigh out the fuel on large scales and load it mercilessly onto the porters' backs.

Down below are the grassy slopes and pine and palm trees of the Botanical Gardens, with glorious flowering rhododendron and magnolia trees, hothouses full of orchids and glasshouses of primroses, primulas and snowdrops. Out past the large Loretto Convent range the slopes of the Happy Valley Tea Plantation. The low, sturdy bushes are planted close together on the steep slopes. Picking time follows the monsoon, so the large red drying and processing factory lies dormant.

The climb back to the upper town is exhausting. We are very short of breath at this altitude. Nehru Road is lined with Victorian chemists and gift shops and traditional men's outfitters. The inside of Glengary's Restaurant has hardly altered since it was used as a small dance hall in the days of the Raj. The open square at the top of the ridge should give views of the surrounding valleys, but it's far too cloudy for that. Nepalese porters appear at the top of steep tracks, some of them barefoot and in shorts

OPPOSITE: THE HAPPY VALLEY TEA PLANTATION

despite the intense cold and clinging damp. We are each wearing three pairs of trousers and all our sweaters. Hire ponies and their owners huddle together under a corrugated shelter.

From the square we follow a track out of the town. Through the shifting clouds we catch glimpses of the valley below, a glint of sunlight on roofs on the far side of the valley, a patch of promising blue sky. . . . In a moment they're gone. The magical trail takes us through misty pine forests, moody Buddhist cemeteries and a half-obscured monastery, till we come out at the village of Ghoom.

Political graffiti is daubed on the walls of the simple houses. The hammer and sickle and red star of the ruling West Bengal Communist Party of India (Marxist) compete with the cries of the Gorkha Liberation Front for an independent (Nepalese) Gorkhaland.

Up a little muddy sideroad the windows of the Tibetan homes are decorated with red, white and green striped awnings. A row of tall white prayer flags lines the approach to Ghoom Monastery. The lofty banners flap noisily in the breeze and merge with the swirling fog. The trees are festooned with strings of old coloured prayer flags. Large prayer wheels encircle the outer wall. Inside the atmosphere is calm and tranquil. An immense and beautiful golden image of the future Buddha dominates the altar. It is guarded by painted carvings of horrific demons and smaller Buddhas in glass cabinets. Books of folded prayers are stacked against the walls. The dark wall paintings have almost disappeared – the effect of age and the burning butter lamps; the air is sweet and thick with their pungent, sticky scent. Small prayer wheels rotate on spindles over lighted candles. At the back, several orange, crested head-dresses rest on long musical horns.

The walk back to Darjeeling is all downhill! In the high season our hotel offers a very full board, with additional 'bed tea' at 6.30 a.m. and 'tiffin' at 4 p.m. We eat Tibetan fried bread and *thupka* (soup) in the Himalaya Restaurant. We buy candles for our room and are in bed by 8 o'clock with all our clothes on. After dark the damp begins to freeze and the lights flicker on and off repeatedly till the town's electricity supply shuts down at 10 o'clock.

12th March – Kathmandu, Nepal

We are sitting on the temple steps in Durbar Square watching the world and his monkey go by. We have come to Nepal for a week's rest, a respite from the rigours of life in India. In front of a three-tiered pagoda stands a little shrine to the ever-popular elephant-headed Ganesh, the god of learning. By another kneels a fine statue of the winged man-bird Garuda, who devours snakes at the door of most of the temples in Kathmandu. Painted wooden statues of Shiva and his consort Parvati lean out of the ornately carved window of a third.

Large white dragon-dogs guard the entrance to the Kumari Devi – the house of the living goddess. The Kumari is chosen at the age of five. During a special ceremony the spirit of the goddess enters her body. She only leaves the house during major festivals. When she reaches puberty she becomes human again and a new goddess must be chosen. It is popularly believed that a man who marries an ex-Kumari will die prematurely. We glimpse her at an open window. It is forbidden to photograph her.

OPPOSITE: DURBAR SQUARE, KATHMANDU

Christopher Cork   1986

Constant streams of people and trishaws snake across the square. The men wear the Nepalese waistcoat and cap; some wear skirts, some shorts. Many hold black umbrellas which protect them from rain or sun, and carry kukris – ceremonial curved daggers – tucked into their waistbands. They lug endless supplies of goods backwards and forwards on carts, on their backs, or on poles across their shoulders – stacked bowls of curd, bulging string bags of shiny pots, piles of block-printed quilts. . . . There are also Nepalese women in brightly coloured saris, Buddhist monks, their heads shaved, in maroon robes, and Hindu sadhus dressed in bright saffron cloths and carrying tridents, the weapon of Shiva. Groups of camera-snapping tourists, a few hippies and familiar faces from India are here too. What a joy it is to be able to sit and watch and draw without attracting an excitable audience full of questions and stares and knees!

The pagoda originated in Nepal. There are more three-tiered examples with erotic carvings in the Palace Square by the giant bell, enormous ceremonial drums and the two huge images of the evil Bhairab, Shiva in his terrifying form. One is black and smeared with colourful sacred pastes; the other is white and even more fearsome. Beyond, in the crowded narrow streets of old Kathmandu, are mask shops, Tibetan rug sellers and run-down temples and shrines. In a street known as Bangemuda there is a block of wood protruding from a wall which has been virtually obliterated by thousands of nails that have been driven into it. This is the Toothache God. If you have a toothache, then take a nail and hammer it into this stump.

To the east of Durbar Square, past the men who sell bamboo flutes, kukri knives and thanka hangings, is Freak Street. A travellers' ghetto in the 1970s, it is still full of café hangouts, secondhand bookshops, overland travel agents and black-market money changers and drug dealers.

We walk past a Shiva temple, whose steps are used by the open-air barbers, and down to the Bagmati River, just a shallow stream forded by makeshift bridges of planks a few inches above the water level. A man is scrubbing a water buffalo and pink pigs are splashing about. On the bank by some

OPPOSITE: BUDDHIST STUPA IN BODHNATH

shrines is a large festering heap of dung and rubbish and gory buffalo carcasses. The place is shimmering with flies. Eagles circle overhead and swoop down one after another, dive-bombing the mound. A little way downstream a body is being cremated. All along the river is the same picture of medieval filth and squalor, just a few minutes walk from European restaurants and the Royal Palace.

Nepal is the only Hindu kingdom in the world. King Birendra came to the throne in 1972 after his father's death, but his coronation did not take place until an auspicious date, in February 1975, had been selected by astrologers. The Nepalese are an immensely superstitious people whose lives are governed by their dogmatic beliefs and practices. The town is full of singing and dancing processions, with wedding feasts going on for days, as this is one of the few auspicious times of the year to get married. Everything closes on Saturday, not because it is a holy day, but because it is an inauspicious day! Mahendra, our new friend, was very upset one day and asked me why I was in mourning: 'But you are wearing your sweater inside out! Has not your mother or father died?'

Nepal's position as the fourth-poorest nation in the world, and lying between India and China, has led to substantial foreign aid from many Western countries. On crossing the border into Nepal, Western influence is immediately evident in Coca-Cola signs and people carrying plastic bags. In India, all goods come wrapped in paper and drinks are sweet, sticky Coke imitations, like 'Thums Up'.

The Nepalese are warm and sincerely friendly. They do all they can to make their guests feel at home, particularly with regard to food. There is an astonishing variety of international cuisine in Kathmandu – a delight after ten weeks in India! Cafés and restaurants proudly boast of their high standards of hygiene: 'All our vegetables are washed in potassium permanganate.' However, throughout our stay in Nepal we are plagued by rumbling stomachs and inauspicious amounts of wind.

In the Kathmandu valley we are spellbound by the magnificent spectacles of the Buddhist temples at Swayambhunath and Bodhnath. The huge white stupas are surmounted by golden towers, with large eyes facing in all four directions, and tangled masses of faded prayer flags. They serve as a stage

NEPALI AND TIBETAN WOMEN

for the fabulous processions of Buddhist pilgrims, who walk round and round in a clockwise direction spinning all the prayer wheels fixed into the walls. Men with wizened faces, narrow eyes, wistful grins and wispy beards, in their big boots and riding trousers, waist sash around their tunics, wide-brimmed leather hats and thick coats – one sleeve on, one off – fumble with their beads, mumble their mantras and spin their little prayer wheels. The Tibetan women wear grey pinafores and colourful striped aprons, bright woollen shawls and a piece of folded cloth on their heads. Many of the women sell jewellery and semi-precious stones from all over the world – lapis lazuli, sea coral, mountain coral, jade, turquoise, amethyst, garnet, yak bone. . . . They speak good English and barter good-humouredly, in stark contrast to the silence of Indian women.

The monks are delighted with Chris's paintings and laugh when they recognize themselves. One invites us to visit his monastery. He tells us it is surrounded by mountains and woods, is beautiful and peaceful, good for painting and we can stay in the monastery. It is four days' walk from here!

The foothills of the Himalayas

24th March – Hardwar

HARDWAR IS ANOTHER very ancient and holy city on the River Ganges, whose people observe the strictest Hindu rules. Not only is it liquor-free and strictly vegetarian, but even eggs are forbidden, since they might contain the beginnings of life.

All along the fast-flowing noisy river people are bathing. Many of them are orange-robed sadhus. Their eccentric painted foreheads mark them out as

OPPOSITE: SADHUS BY THE GANGES AT HARDWAR

SACRED COWS AND CROWS

followers of Vishnu or Shiva. After their daily purifying bathe they re-adorn their brows lovingly in vermilion, ochre and white with the aid of little mirrors. There are more, and more varied, sadhus here than we have seen anywhere else. Some look calm and peaceful while others look wild, with matted hair, large tridents, scanty clothing, powdery white (or even blue) bodies, fierce make-up and 'witch doctor' jewellery. The most highly venerated ascetics wear no clothing at all and cover themselves with ashes from sacred fires. One lilac holy man stands up to his chest in the freezing waters meditating for hours. Some set up 'shop' with nuts and beads and conch shells on sheets.

They offer mantras, talismans and promises to heal illnesses and exorcize evil spirits in return for alms.

Each day at dusk people gather on the Har-ki-Pauri ghat for the *arti*, the evening worship. Har-ki-Pauri is the most sacred ghat as it marks the precise spot where the Ganges leaves the mountains and enters the plains. It also boasts an impression in stone of Vishnu's footprint. Many groups of pilgrims from different parts of the country bathe and puja together. They hold on to each other in pairs and bounce up and down in the swift-flowing stream, whose surface is littered with colourful offerings floating away on the current – pieces of fabric, coconuts, flower garlands, pages from prayerbooks, even banknotes. Rajasthani Bhil women in their brightly patterned skirts and veils openly bare their breasts as they wash in the river. Women from other communities are extremely adept at squatting carefully and washing themselves discreetly.

The great Hindu festival of Kumbh Mela attracts a most spectacular religious gathering. In a legendary battle between the gods and the demons for possession of an urn (*kumbh*) containing a divine nectar ensuring immortality, four drops of the ambrosia were spilt on the earth at Allahabad, Hardwar, Nasik and Ujjain. The mythical struggle lasted 12 days and a god's day is a human's year. So the Kumbh Mela comes to each town every 12 years, rotating between the cities every three years. This year the Kumbh Mela is coming to Hardwar and huge tent cities are being erected all along the far bank of the river and in every spare space to accommodate the invasion by half a million pilgrims which will swell the town to 35 times its normal size. The most important bathing dates are posted up by the river and fall throughout April. We tour some competition tents where gross and distasteful painted mud and straw statues of the gods are being constructed. A large elephant is chained unhappily to a tree outside. He angrily hurls sticks and branches at passers-by.

25th March – Rishikesh
Rishikesh is surrounded by hills. The banks of the Ganges are studded with religious institutions, temples and ashrams – lodging houses for pilgrims who come to study yoga and other disciplines or

who are passing through on their way to shrines further upstream.

Across the river is like Pilgrims' Pleasureland. Trashy souvenir shops and spiritual guide book stalls serve the ashrams and lodges where the pilgrims live in tiny cells. The well-kept peaceful gardens of the Ved Niketan compound are peopled by wandering tribes of sadhus sporting a wide variety of orange apparel and painted footwear. The constant reading through loudspeakers ceases with the ringing of bells and all the orange folk pick up their sticks and tridents and traipse off to their transcendental meditation, or whatever, like a band of fairy-tale goblins.

Holy men wander along the river with their staffs and begging pots. Most are simple men who choose to find god through ascetic meandering. Tens of thousands of them walk India's roads. People respect them, give them food and seek their prayers. Some serve as gurus – counsellors and spiritual advisers. Through the trees we spot the transcendental meditation school of Rishikesh's most famous guru, Maharishi Mahesh Yogi, visited by the Beatles in the sixties.

26th March – Holi Festival in Chandigarh

We stand on the hotel balcony looking at the row of houses opposite. Each slightly different in their angular design, they resemble European 'Moderne' houses of the twenties and thirties. This is Chandigarh, capital of the Punjab, constructed in the 1950s to a plan by Le Corbusier.

From the flat rooftops young boys surreptitiously and accurately waterbomb passing cyclists. The riders shrug it off, for today is Holi, a national public holiday marking the arrival of spring. People traditionally celebrate this high-spirited Hindu festival by throwing coloured water and powder at each other. It is the one day on which no holds are barred and customary caste divisions can be transgressed by the joyfully riotous behaviour which symbolizes the Holi spirit of brotherhood and friendship. For several days children have been practising their aim, lobbing thin plastic bags of water into crowded thoroughfares. So far we have escaped a soaking, but we wonder what our fate will be today!

OPPOSITE: THE FESTIVAL OF HOLI

At 9 a.m. we make a dash for the bus station. It is already dazzlingly bright and hot. Set back off the streets of downtown Chandigarh are long rows of furniture stores, restaurants and 'English wine' (whisky) shops. At one roundabout cyclists and motorists dodge round a body lying on the ground. Was it a traffic accident or a shooting incident? There has been so much violence in the Punjab recently. Armed police man several of the junctions. The suburbs are laid out on a massive scale – wide roads, huge roundabouts and enormous plots of land, many of them still empty wastegrounds.

The 'luxury v.d.o.' bus to Simla is certainly very comfortable. We feel even more relaxed when the video refuses to work, despite much fiddling by a mechanic. We are relieved to be spared the aural and visual assault of another Bombay epic melodrama with chubby heroes, Rasputin-like 'baddies' who can summon up evil snakes with a frown, song and dance scenes involving amateur 'trick' photography, and energetic and totally erratic editing throughout.

The revelry outside provides much better entertainment. In every town we pass through the bus is 'held up' and bombarded with coloured water and powder. Everybody, young and old, is absolutely covered in splashes of red, blue, yellow and green. They hurl their powders then hug each other to rub it in. Shopkeepers and stall holders sit dutifully at their posts with pink hair and blue faces.

27th March – Simla

Before Independence, Simla was known as the 'summer capital' of India. When the heat on the plains became unbearable the government officials would escape to the cool mountain air of Simla, strung out along a crescent-shaped ridge at an altitude of 7000 ft. Many books have been written about the summer social antics of this most important British hill station.

The town still has a cosy English country atmosphere with mock-Tudor buildings, bandstands, English churches, rather terribly awfully English shops, a Gaiety Theatre, Rivoli Cinema, a parade ground and an open-air winter ice-skating rink ('the only one of its kind in Asia').

At the beginning of the Mall, from which all

PADDY FIELDS

vehicles and Indians were banned until the First World War, is the South Indian Coffee Shop. Downstairs is like a men's club, full of smoke and chat, heads bobbing sideways at shoulder level in that inimitable Indian gesture indicating 'yes' or 'I understand' and murmurings of *'acha, acha . . .'*. Upstairs holiday-making families are packed round the chairs and tables blocking the tall mantelpiece and 19th-century fireplace. The waiters wear heavy green uniforms with red sashes and cummerbunds and frilly turbans.

We find the town very sedate and boring, resting on its British laurels which have long since rotted. All day long, but particularly in the late afternoon, Sikh and middle-class Hindu tourists *passagiata* along the Mall. Their paths are criss-crossed by short, sturdy Himachal porters. They wear round felt caps with plain velvet or woven borders and carry every load imaginable on their sacking-covered backs. Tibetan women in striped aprons sell shawls. Children go for pony rides across the parade ground. From the ridge the narrow streets

OPPOSITE: WORKERS' DEMONSTRATION IN SIMLA

fall away steeply to the smoking corrugated roof-tops of the local bazaars and houses.

Simla is the state capital of Himachal Pradesh and today there is a peaceful demonstration of workers waving banners, chanting slogans and making speeches outside the state offices, which are amply protected by squads of riot police with lathis and basket-weave shields at the ready.

The State Museum is a quaint building in pleasant gardens up a steep hill with fine scenic views. The collection of miniatures from the 16th-century Northern schools depict everyday Indian life – domestic scenes, craftsmen at work, people washing and pampering their bodies, celebrating Holi – which has barely changed in the intervening centuries. We recognize the same traditions, the same dress styles, hair styles, moustache styles. . . .

In the evening, back in our hotel, we wrap up in extra blankets and turn on the telly. Indian TV is appalling – a series of simplistic melodramas with bad overacting and outdated film techniques. The news in English is on every evening at 9.30. It tells of increasing violence in the Punjab. Several towns are under extended curfews. The local leader of the

CPI (Marxist) and his bodyguard were shot dead on Thursday. On Friday, 13 Hindus were gunned down by Sikh extremists on motorbikes disguised as policemen. There are also curfews in towns in Gujarat and Uttar Pradesh.

1st April – Manali

It's a beautiful clear morning as we look out of the window at the wooded snowy hills and peaks that surround this little resort at the top of the Kulu Valley. We don as many clothes as we can and head for the new Tibetan monastery. The Tibetans live in sheds round a stupa draped in prayer flags and bordered by prayer stones painted with the mystical symbol 'Om'.

We cross the fast-flowing river, passing yellow fields of mustard. Pink and white buds are beginning to blossom in the orchards. The end of the valley is blocked by steep, snowy, forested hillsides whose rocky peaks are hidden in cloud and mist.

Up a little track are the natural hot sulphur baths of Vashisht. We enjoy a wonderful 20-minute soak

OPPOSITE: TIBETAN HOUSES IN MANALI

in a big luxurious tiled tub. When we re-emerge it starts to snow. A little way further on is Vashisht village, an extremely picturesque collection of sturdy houses with chunky carved wooden doorways decorated with golden designs and bundles of leaves. The animals live snugly on the ground floor. The upper floor houses the family and is supplemented by a deep verandah on all sides, suspended from the roof timbers. Pots and tools are stored up here and the fair-skinned women in brightly woven tunics and headscarves work the looms. Children play at their feet with the wool. An enormously heavy, haphazard arrangement of thick slates covers the roof.

We sit in a café opposite the village school. The children arrive with their slates and chalk. One teacher moves between the four classrooms conducting the groups in their rote learning like a circus-act plate spinner. Painted on the outside wall among a tangle of Hindi script is the philosophy 'Art is Life'. We sip our Bournvitas and watch the taxi-loads of young Indian honeymooners stepping out in their silk and leather finery and rubber galoshes. They visit the temple, wash their feet in the hot spring, rush back to the taxi's cassette player and whizz off back to Manali.

We walk back through the woods – tall conifers, short grass, wild iris in bud, flocks of sheep and goats. We eat in a restaurant with a warming central stove and Pink Floyd tapes. We resist the 'Spacial Dinner – surved tea or coffee, soop, stake, mass patato, apple cramble with custered' and instead order 'scrimbled eggs' and pasta.

2nd April – Manali to Dharmsala

We catch the 6 a.m. bus in the pouring rain, freezing cold and black dark. The roof of the bus leaks. The aromatic scent of the burning incense by the shrine on the dashboard wafts down the aisle. The narrow valley broadens out a little as we descend to Kulu. The valley floor is very fertile here, planted with apple and fruit orchards, rice paddies and wheatfields. Well-tended terraces rise up the lower slopes below the forested hills and snow-covered rocky peaks. The exit from the valley is through a precipitous gorge above the fast-flowing Beas River. The torrential rain causes little waterfalls to cascade down the slopes between the palm trees.

Halfway down we stop at a gaudy little temple while a devotee climbs aboard, distributing white sweets. Some people give coins in return.

A party of four honeymooning couples insist on having a wild time. They giggle and howl the whole day long. They don't all sit together but spread themselves out along half the bus. They dress in typical Indian tourist fashion. The men are in woollen balaclavas and/or large-brimmed leatherette hats, too-tight trousers, big-heeled shoes or boots, clashing patterned shirts and jumpers. The women wear bright colourful saris or shalwar camise (tunic and trousers), two cardigans each, grey or beige woollen socks, and flip-flops or gold sling-backs with big heels. The honeymoon gang borrow a reggae cassette from an Italian boy and play it loudly. One of them dances erotic disco style in the crowded aisle while the others hoot and guffaw. When they have finished they hand back the tape and ask: 'Is this Lionel Richie?'

We pass several groups of beautiful young cows in embroidered sack coats, huge flocks of sheep and a local god being taken out in procession on a palanquin. As we approach Dharmsala the bus

BOY ON A BUFFALO

swings off down a gentle green valley to Kangra. The bus station is full of different religious groups. One sect is dressed all in bright yellow with yellow turbans. An orange man sits with a group of women dressed all in red. We head back towards the endless line of snowy mountains turning peach-pink in the setting sun.

At last we reach Dharmsala – a sleepy, straggling ex-British hill station. The snow-topped rock wall of the Dhauladhar range looms majestically behind the ridges above. We share a taxi with four Tibetans up the 6-mile winding hill road through beautiful woods to the tiny Tibetan hamlet of McLeod Ganj.

4th April – McLeod Ganj

Before we left England people asked us: 'Why India?' 'To find ourselves,' as people had said in the sixties, we joked. Now we find ourselves surrounded by Westerners of all ages immersed in this spiritual quest. Eastern religions still exert a strong pull on the 'lost souls' from the West.

The little village is crowded with students of Buddhism and Tibetan culture, for it was here that the Dalai Lama and his followers settled after the Chinese invasion of Tibet. There are many Western monks and nuns dressed in saffron and maroon robes and with shaved heads. The hotels, lodges and private homes are booked up by people attending courses on meditation and Buddhist philosophy. Astrologers advertise their services on shop walls. We meet people everywhere who've been staying in ashrams following different leaders and their teachings. 'Have you seen a monk called Ken?' a girl asks Chris one day in a café. In another sits a group of young English people all wearing hand-knitted bright Tibetan sweaters, discussing their course textbook, *Wisdom, Energy and Theology*. 'I don't like losing control of my mind!' exclaims the American 'sufi dancer'. Everyone is discussing their ailments and swapping cures and remedies as prescribed by their Tibetan doctors. The physical price of enlightenment is high in this spiritual health farm. We rename this town 'McLeod 9'. We are happy here on the eve of our departure for home!

A short walk along the winding lane down to Dharmsala stands the pretty little English Church of St John in the Wilderness. Built in the shadows of tall fir trees, the simple Gothic structure is being

carefully restored. Plaques inside tell of officers dying from wounds received in action and climbing accidents, remembered by their widows, fellow officers and the regiment. In the graveyard alongside the monument to Lord Elgin are buried many children of the Raj, and a few young Westerners from recent years. In another section lie the victims of an earthquake on this very same day, 4th April, in 1905.

Snowy peaks, so clear and inviting, peep over the steep forested hills and ridges behind the town. The pine woods are a gorgeous place to walk. Delicate butterflies and bright red humming-birds flit backwards and forwards among the large rhododendron trees in brilliant red bloom. In a clearing by a banyan tree we come across the tomb of a rinpoche (an elevated Buddhist title). The Tibetans and the Nepalese plant banyan and pipul trees together on stone platforms to provide shade for travellers. The construction of the platform is more than a public service, it is the joining of the two trees in sacred wedlock.

LEFT: THE BLUE SADHU

We spot a bright blue face in the undergrowth. We investigate and discover a sadhu, dressed up as Shiva, putting the finishing touches to his make-up. He is painted blue all over. A rubber cobra which spits water is woven into his long tangled black wig. He wears a gold paper necklace with red flowers and a leopard-skin cloth tied around his loins. He carries a red trident and a golden pot. His dark brown legs show through the shiny blue paint. He has two thumbs on his left hand. He poses for us austerely. He looks magnificent.

A very steep path plunges down to Dharmsala, passing the monastery, the Dalai Lama's residence and the Tibetan library. We are drawn towards the monastery by the sounds of horns and bells. Buddhists are very open about their religion and welcome people warmly at their monasteries and temples. An important ceremony is in progress behind the temple. Rows of monks are seated on the floor. The front row wear ornate silk cloaks and black and red hats. They are flanked by young monks blowing on long horns. An elderly monk on a wooden dais presides over the burning of offerings. A novice monk holds a black umbrella to shade him from the sun. Plate-loads of rice and beans and other foodstuffs are passed to him from a fully-laden side table. He scatters them on to the fire below him. Chanting and singing accompanies the performance. As each offering is completed bells are rung, little drums are rattled and blasts sound from the horns. The litany continues until the table is bare. The celebrant uses an enormously long ladle to pour melted butter over the sacred flames to ensure thorough burning. Once the ceremony is over the monks quickly depart and all that remains is the smouldering fire.

An American woman, dressed all in black and looking like a Sichuan peasant, appears mumbling loudly and 'knowingly' about the inscrutable rituals. She is perplexed. Which is the most auspicious side of the smouldering fire from which to remove ashes to help heal her bandaged foot and to share with Tibetan nomads on her return journey through Tibet to Beijing, where she lectures on Western architecture? She tells us we are fortunate to be here today, for this is the last day of an annual

OPPOSITE: BUDDHIST MEDICINE CEREMONY

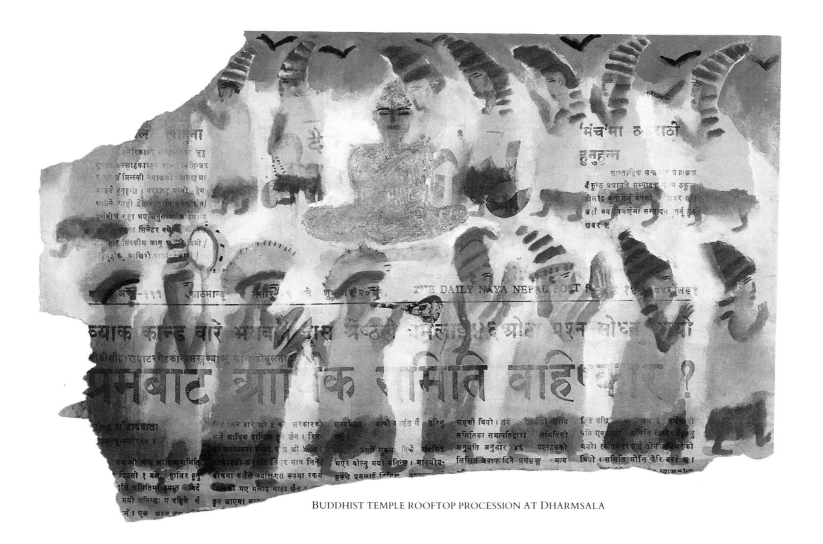

BUDDHIST TEMPLE ROOFTOP PROCESSION AT DHARMSALA

14-day ceremony to prepare powerful holy medicines which will be distributed throughout the Buddhist world. She tells us this fortnight of puja always brings on a big storm – never fails! His Holiness the Dalai Lama himself was in attendance yesterday. The concluding ceremony will begin at 1 o'clock inside the temple. The bright sunny morning begins to cloud over.

On the lawns the student monks are practising their debating skills in the traditional ways, unchanged since the ninth century. Single monks sit on the ground and make salient points which question the essentials of Buddhist philosophy. Small groups surround them and in turn must argue forcibly in favour of their teachings. They make their points tellingly by smacking their hands together loudly in front of the questioner's face, like an American football pitcher. It is arguably the most aggressive action they indulge in (except in a bus station).

The temple contains several beautiful Buddha images, photographs of Buddhas which remain in Tibet, and relics recovered from statues destroyed by the Chinese. We are excluded from the temple for the final ritual. We can see nothing, only hear the music – fantastic booms and sirens from the large horns, bagpipe-like wails from the smaller ones, bells and drums, chants and prayers and the deep droning of 'Om…mmmmmmm'. A curtain is removed from the doorway and we are able to witness the rites taking place within the sanctuary. These involve the donning and removal of large orange-crested caps; the presentation and subsequent destruction of a multitude of coloured butter sculptures decorated like Easter eggs; a change of head-dress to tall red and white hooped caps; and finally a procession up onto the temple roof to the golden Wheel of Law.

By now a cold wind has blown up and the sky has turned black and menacing. Packs of scavenging crows caw loudly and swoop down, picking at the offerings placed on the roof. The mountains have disappeared in fierce enveloping storm clouds and large drops of rain begin to fall heavily from the sky.

Drawing in India

by Christopher Corr

INDIA HAS SO MUCH to record: overwhelming crowds, chaos, noise, beggars, animals and dust everywhere, brilliant colours, astonishing traffic-filled streets, temples and shrines, gurus and sadhus. . . . I spent the first week in a daze asking myself 'How do I draw all this?'. And how DO you draw all this?

Drawing in India is hard work. Crowds mass around you quickly, blocking your view. People touch and feel your paper. Those on the outside push because they can't see what's going on. And

NASIK ROAD RAILWAY STATION

you sit in the middle of it all getting hotter and more fed up. I felt like a fairground side-show and I suppose that's what I looked like.

The only time I ever saw anyone else drawing in the street was in Simla. Near a Hindu temple sat a boy with deformed hands (no fingers and twisted wrists) drawing in coloured biros in an exercise book. His pictures, mostly with religious themes, were very clearly drawn. People threw him small coins. He looked happy.

Drawing is not intrusive like a camera can be. It allows you to make intimate pictures of ordinary life. Many people treated me warmly, seeing me draw their country. Sometimes one of the crowd

WEL - COME TO INDIA

would act as 'controller' and keep my view clear. In Udaipur, while I drew a busy street scene in front of the Jagdish temple, a stallholder selling posters of religious gods and musclemen (their earthly counterparts?) looked after me all afternoon, keeping onlookers at bay and supplying me with cups of sweet tea. At Varanasi station on a dimly lit platform another man shone his torch on my sketchbook so I could see what I was painting.

A lot of people asked to be drawn or 'photographed' as they called it. They would stand right in front of whatever I was drawing and give me instructions: 'Make sure you put in my watch!' 'Are you painting my moustaches?' I quickly learnt about Indian status symbols and vanity. I drew a lot of 'posers' to begin with but later on I was less obliging.

At Victoria Terminus, Bombay, with trains coming and going, crowds pushing, vendors shouting, porters carrying great loads on their heads, the army preening itself, combing hair and eyebrows, gazing into mirrors, the porters lined up to be painted, tying their red turbans specially and showing off their official brass armplate licences.

Not everybody wanted to be drawn. A traffic cop in Indore became very angry with me when I drew him. Sometimes kids threw stones at us, others pushed and shoved and poked and smudged and did everything they could to be irritating.

I learnt to work discreetly wherever possible, seeking out vantage points inaccessible to crowds, and hoped I wouldn't be noticed. In Jaipur, the 'pink city', I rented a balcony for an afternoon from a shrewd woman, enabling me to draw a chaotic street scene in blissful solitude. In Varanasi we hired boats to record life along the Ganges in sounds and pictures.

India is never boring. It is an overwhelming and exhausting place with so much going on all around. It's full of mysterious customs and unanswered questions, strange and beautiful sights, dazzlingly vivid colours and incredible grace and elegance set against primitive backdrops. Anything can and does happen. A cow painted pink with huge blue horns will amble by eating a newspaper, a monkey will bound out of the dust and swipe some unprotected food. You might find yourself, as we did, sharing a railway carriage on a ten-hour journey through the deserts of Rajasthan with a tone-deaf snake charmer and his entourage of two wives, seven bored kids and a snake in a basket. A naked sadhu might stop and offer to reveal to you the meaning of life and the mysteries of the universe . . . or he might just want the price of a cup of *chai*.

Everybody wants to talk to you and find out all about you and your impressions of India. 'What is your service?' they ask. 'I'm an artist,' I reply. 'A craftsman, sculptor, musician, dancer. . . ?' 'A traditional artist? Do you paint on wood, cloth, ivory. . . ?' When I say I'm a modern artist they look dubious and a little suspicious. I met other artists and craftsmen while drawing – a primitive toy maker from Uttar Pradesh, a Gujarati artist who painted on glass, a blacksmith who embossed pictures in tin, a mask maker in Maharashtra. They showed me their workshops and their work. Art in India is largely a routine job as far as I can see. It is tied to religion and historical legend. Personal expression plays little part in it. The 'modern' art in India I like best is the brash film posters and shop sign paintings.

Working in India forced me to draw more on the move than I'd ever done before – in trains, on buses, even walking, I sketched as I went along, assembling pictures from the changing scenes around me. I'm more interested in making an informative atmospheric picture than in capturing a specific place at one instant in time.

Indian traffic is for me the most exciting spectacle to draw. It's noisy and colourful and full of surprises, an astonishing parade like a circus finale of vehicles and carts pulled by animals and men and all piled high with a fantastic variety of 'goods'. You never know what will come along next.

As I drew an extravagantly costumed Sikh procession in Indore a young man said to me, 'And how will you picturize this – systematically?' How can I picturize India? Systematically? Im-possible!

index

Page numbers in *italic* refer to illustrations

a

Agra 70–3
Ahmadabad 28–35, *30, 37*
Ajanta 20–3
Anointing a shrine *49*
Archaeological dig at Fatehpur Sikri *75*

b

Bathing ghats at Dwarka *44*
Bathing in the Ganges at Varanasi *79*
Bhil women 55, *56*
Bhuj 47–50
Blue sadhu *119*
Bombay 6–11
Boy on a buffalo *117*
Buddhist medicine ceremony *121*
  monks and Tibetans spinning prayer wheels *95*
  stupa in Bodhnath *101*
  temple rooftop procession at Dharmsala *122*
Bullocks turning a water wheel, Diu *39*

c

Chandigarh 108–10
Crossing the plains *13*

d

Dalsing Sarai in Bihar *92*
Darjeeling 94–8
Delhi 71, 74–9, *76*, 85–6

Desert farms in the Rann of Kutch *48*
  village *43*
Dharmsala 116–18, *122*
Diu 38–9, *39*
Down by the tank *82*
Dudh-wallahs by Nakki Lake *54*
Durbar Square, Kathmandu *97*
Dwarka *44*, 45–7, *47*

e

Evening scrub *46*
Evening time in Mandu village *27*

f

Farmer and storks *51*
Fatehpur Sikri 73–4, *75*
Festival of Holi 108–10, *109*
Fishermen *81*
Fortune-teller and his green parrot *33*
Fruit and veg. market *11, 64*

g

Goatherd in Saurashtra *29*
Green field in the Thar Desert *53*

h

Hanging up fish to dry *40*
Happy Valley Tea Plantation *96*
Hardwar 104–7, *105*
Holi festival 108–10, *109*

j

Jaipur 67–9, *67, 68*
Jaisalmer 60–7, *62, 64*

k

Kathmandu 97, 98–103, *101*
Khultabad street *18*

m

Manali *114*, 115–16
Mandu 25, *27*
Market stalls *11, 14, 15, 64*
McLeod Ganj 118–23
Mount Abu 52–5
Mud houses in the Thar Desert *66*

n

Nasik 12–19, *15*
Nasik Road railway station *125*
Nepali and Tibetan women *103*
New Delhi traffic *76*
Night time in Ahmadabad *30*

o

Old Delhi railway station *71*

p

Paddy fields *88, 111*
Palace of Winds, Jaipur *68*
  Royal, at Jaisalmer *62*
Palitana 35–8
Pan stall *9*
Porbanda *45*
Puja at the bathing ghats *80*
Pushkar 58–60

r

Railway station *61, 71, 125*
Rishikesh 107–8
Road menders and sacred cow *34*
Royal Palace at Jaisalmer *62*

s

Sacred cow(s) and calf *32*

  and crows *106*
  and hoopoe *21*
  and road menders *34*
  in an embroidered coat *title page*
Sadhu(s) *105, 119*
Saint with leopards temple, Bihar *91*
Saurashtran men at Ahmadabad bus station *37*
Simla 110–15, *112*
Street bath *78*
Street in Jaipur *67*
  in Khultabad *18*

t

Taj Mahal *72*
Temples in Ujjain *22*
  on the beach, Dwarka *47*
Thar Desert *53, 63, 66*
Thieving monkeys at the railway station *61*
Tibetan(s) and Buddhist monks spinning prayer wheels *95*
  and Nepali women *103*
  houses in Manali *114*
Traffic *76, 85*

u

Udaipur 57–8
Ujjain 22, 23–6

v

Varanasi 79–85, *79*
Village in Bihar *87*

w

Women dhobis *16*
Women washing at the lake *59*
Workers' demonstration in Simla *112*